The Book of Krishna

The Book of
Krishna

PAVAN K. VARMA

PENGUIN BOOKS

PENGUIN BOOKS

Published by the Penguin Group

Penguin Books India Pvt. Ltd, 11 Community Centre, Panchsheel Park, New Delhi 110 017, India

Penguin Group (USA) Inc., 375 Hudson Street, New York, New York 10014, USA

Penguin Group (Canada), 90 Eglinton Avenue East, Suite 700, Toronto, Ontario, M4P 2Y3, Canada (a division of Pearson Penguin Canada Inc.)

Penguin Books Ltd, 80 Strand, London WC2R 0RL, England

Penguin Ireland, 25 St Stephen's Green, Dublin 2, Ireland (a division of Penguin Books Ltd)

Penguin Group (Australia), 250 Camberwell Road, Camberwell, Victoria 3124, Australia (a division of Pearson Australia Group Pty Ltd)

Penguin Group (NZ), 67 Apollo Drive, Rosedale, North Shore 0632, New Zealand (a division of Pearson New Zealand Ltd)

Penguin Group (South Africa) (Pty) Ltd, 24 Sturdee Avenue, Rosebank, Johannesburg 2196, South Africa

Penguin Books Ltd, Registered Offices: 80 Strand, London WC2R 0RL, England

First published in Viking by Penguin Books India 2001
Published in Penguin Books 2009

Text copyright © Pavan K. Varma 2001
Illustrations copyright © Penguin Books India 2001
Illustrations by K.G. Narendra Babu

All rights reserved

10 9 8 7 6 5 4 3 2 1

ISBN 9780143067634

Typeset in Sabon by Mantra Virtual Services, New Delhi
Printed at De Unique, New Delhi

Contents

Preface

Parts of this book, written specially for the Penguin India series on short biographies of Hindu gods and goddesses, are derived from my earlier book, *Krishna: The Playful Divine*. The writing of both these books has been for me an intensely rewarding experience. It provided me with an opportunity to rediscover Hindu religion and mythology, its loftiness, its pragmatism, its sublime sensitivities and its daring resolve to imbue reverence with humour, passion and tenderness.

In any society, individual autonomy acquires meaning only if it is based on at least a basic knowledge of the conditioning and contextual factors that constitute the inheritance of that society. The malaise of our times is that, in many respects, we, as a nation, are adrift from our own moorings. Forms, symbols and rituals remain, without an understanding of the substance, meanings and precepts that animate them. All the more reason for us to once again familiarize ourselves with the bequest of Krishna.

My thanks are due to David Davidar and Ravi Singh. I hope this edition will help more people understand India's most popular deity.

Introduction

Krishna is perhaps the most popular Hindu divinity. From time immemorial he has captured the imagination of the Hindu mind, and, in his own inimitable way, provided succour to millions of believers. The purpose of this book is to try and explore the persistence of his appeal. Beyond a point, faith, reinforced over centuries, is not a matter of analysis. But it is often possible to desegregate and examine the components that account for the strength of its hold and the richness of its contents. Krishna is an extremely lovable god. He is a personal saviour. His divinity is accessible and his personality has human resonances in such plenitude that, almost immediately, the gap between the mortal and the immortal is bridged. Unlike other incarnations of Vishnu, Krishna is regarded as a purna avatar, the complete incarnation, encapsulating in himself the entire canvas of emotions and attributes that constitute the ideal human personality.

A study of Krishna is important also for the insight it provides into the concept of divinity in the Hindu ethos. To a foreigner, or a non-Hindu, the escapades of the child Kanha, or the dalliances of Murari, could appear a trifle bizarre. But the attraction of Krishna lies precisely in this exuberance of his multifaceted personality. The gopis adore him as Bal Gopal, the irrepressibly mischievous yet innocent child; they love him as Shyam, the dark and bewitching flute player;

the Pandavas and Kauravas vie to have him on their side in the Mahabharata; the percipience of his upadesha gives salvation to Arjuna; and the lure of his personal charm enables millions to alleviate the engulfing ennui of their lives. The godhood of Krishna was never supposed to be put on a remote and aloof pedestal. The love and reverence he invoked was never meant to be monochromatic. I have often felt that a Hindu lives in a kind of harmonious schizophrenia, wherein the vision of the Almighty, serene and beyond all categories at one level, hardly diminishes this joyous and even extravagant humanization, at another. To the Hindu mind, divinity is not necessarily a hostage to conventional yardsticks of behaviour. It is meaningful for the images it evokes, for the emotions it releases, for the ends it achieves and for the sheer joy and bliss it symbolizes and guarantees.

Child

On the eighth day of the waning half of the lunar month of Bhadrapada (August–September), the horizons were suffused with a new joy. The fires in the hearths of holy men burnt without smoke. A gentle wind blew, the sky was clear, and the stars shone with unusual brilliance. Rivers, their waters sweet and clear, flowed with serenity, the lakes were full of lotuses, the trees were in splendid blossom, and the waves of the sea made music. As the midnight hour approached, it appeared as if all of creation was drenched in the moonlight. And then, as the glorious moment arrived, the earth and the oceans trembled. The gods showered flower petals upon the earth. The notes of the divine 'dundubhi' rent the air. Heavenly spirits and nymphs—gandharvas and apsaras—danced and sang in abandon. There was a burst of light as fires, long dead, rose high in obeisance. A deep thunder, awesome like the roar of the ocean, rumbled across the clear sky. There fell a hush, and Krishna, the protector of the world, the incarnation of Vishnu, eighth child of Devaki, son of Vasudeva, and nephew of the wicked king Kamsa, was born.

His birth was not an accident. Prithvi, Mother Earth, had suffered long from the depredations of evil and wicked men and women, who had forgotten dharma, the law of righteousness. Crime and persecution had become rampant and, in dread, religion and justice had fled. Kamsa, who ruled Mathura, having usurped the throne from his good father, Ugrasena, was foremost among the wicked. His cruelty was matched only by his arrogance and lack of repentance. Unable to bear this state of affairs any more, Prithvi, assuming the form of a cow, went to Mount Meru, where the gods—Indra, Shiva and Brahma—had assembled. Hearing her tale of woe, Brahma approached Vishnu as he lay on his serpent couch in the Milky Sea, and begged the limitless author of creation, preservation and destruction to come to the assistance of Prithvi. Vishnu, ever compassionate, agreed. Plucking out two of his hairs, one black and one white, he said: 'This, my black hair, shall be incarnate in the eighth child of the wife of Vasudeva, Devaki, and shall kill Kamsa, who is none other than the great demon Kalenemi.' The white hair, the Lord said, would also be born to Devaki, as her seventh child. Together the two would kill the demons and rid the world of its accumulated evil.

Kamsa became aware of his impending fate on the day of the marriage of his sister Devaki to Vasudeva, son of Sura, an important chieftain of the clan of the Yadava, who were descendants of Yadu, son of King Yayati of the Lunar race. As Vasudeva prepared to take his newly wedded wife home, a celestial voice proclaimed: 'Kamsa, you fool, this woman, your sister, will be the cause of your death. Her eighth son will kill you.' In a flash, Kamsa's sword left its scabbard to kill

Devaki, but Vasudeva pleaded with him to spare his wife's life on condition that he would hand over to him all their sons. Kamsa relented and put Vasudeva and Devaki in prison under heavy guard. There Devaki in time had six sons, all of whom Kamsa mercilessly put to death. Devaki's seventh son was declared to be a miscarriage, but in reality, Lord Vishnu had commanded the goddess Yoganidra, who is described in the Vishnu Purana as 'the great illusory energy of Vishnu, by whom, as utter ignorance, the whole world is beguiled', to transfer the embryo—formed of a portion of Sesha, the many-headed serpent, which was a part of Vishnu—to the womb of Rohini, another wife of Vasudeva, residing in nearby Gokula. This child was Balarama, also known as Sankarsana, since he was extracted from his mother's womb.

The Lord himself became incarnate in the eighth conception of Devaki. Yoganidra simultaneously entered the womb of Yasoda, the wife of Nanda, the gentle leader of the cowherd settlement at Gokula. A day after Devaki—now luminous from the lustre of the embryo she carried—gave birth to Krishna, Yasoda delivered a girl, who was none other than the goddess Yoganidra. Vasudeva picked up his infant son and carried him out of the prison, whose guards, under the mysterious influence of Yoganidra, had fallen into a deep sleep. It was raining, but Sesha spread his hoods over father and

son to accord protection. The deep and turbulent
Yamuna rose momentarily to be blessed by the feet of
the child in Vasudeva's hands, and then fell low, rising
not above the knees of Vasudeva. Across the Yamuna
Vasudeva reached Gokula, placed the infant Krishna
next to Yasoda and carried her daughter safely back to
Kamsa's prison. Under the powerful influence of
Yoganidra, neither Gokula, nor Yasoda, nor Nanda,
nor Kamsa's guards, knew of what had occurred.

On being informed that Devaki had given birth to
her eighth child, Kamsa immediately went to the prison,
and ignoring the piteous entreaties of Devaki, dashed
the child against a stone. But no sooner had the child
touched the stone than it rose into the sky and expanded
into a gigantic figure, having eight arms, each wielding
a formidable weapon. This terrific being laughed aloud,
and said to Kamsa, 'What avails it thee, Kamsa, to have
buried me to the ground? He is born who shall kill thee,
the mighty one amongst the gods, who was formerly
thy destroyer. Now quickly secure him, and provide for
thine own welfare.' Thus having spoken, the goddess
vanished before the eyes of Kamsa.

Kamsa, in much perturbation, went into conference
with his advisers. As a protective measure, he ordered
that a full search be made for all children less than a
year old, and that they all be killed. Meanwhile, Gokula
woke up, as if from a trance, to the joyous news that

Yasoda had given birth to a son. Krishna, Lord of Lords, began his incarnate life in the humble abode of the cowherd chief Nanda, in the sylvan surroundings of Gokula.

The early years of Krishna's life were spent in the pastoral setting of Gokula and nearby Vrindavan. The cattle herders' commune provides the backdrop to Krishna's childhood adventures, described in the early texts—the *Harivamsa*, the Vishnu Purana and the Bhagavata Purana—which deal with his life. (The extracts from the *Harivamsa* in this work have been taken from the lyrical translation by Francis G. Hutchinson, *Young Krishna*; those from the Vishnu Purana from the scholarly and pioneering translation by H.H. Wilson and those from the Bhagavata Purana unless otherwise indicated from the summarized but comprehensive rendering of its text by Kamala Subramanian, *Srimad Bhagavatam*.)

The story of the child Krishna's victory over the serpent Kaliya is a particularly popular one. No play or ballet on the life of Krishna is complete without the enactment of this dramatic feat. In the waters of the Yamuna, as it flowed along the shores of Vrindavan, there was, so the lore goes, one viciously noxious pool.

The *Harivamsa,* in typical poetic hyperbole, describes the pool thus:

> Even a God could scarcely have crossed it. This pool was as deep and blank as a motionless sea. Its surface burned with the brilliance of a bushfire. Its stagnant depths were impenetrable, like the sky when thick with clouds. It was difficult to walk along its shore, which was pitted by large snake holes. The air above was empty of birds. Fumes rose from the water like smoke from a putrid fire.

In this pool lived the king of nagas (serpents), the five-headed Kaliya. One day Krishna and the gopas tending the herd strayed near Kaliya's abode. Some of the gopas and cows were inadvertently affected by the pool's toxic waters. Krishna then climbed a kadambha tree stretching out over the pool and fearlessly jumped into the deadly waters to do battle with Kaliya. Kaliya, the Bhagavata Purana states, 'caught hold of Krishna and wound his entire length round the form of the young boy; with his five heads he spat his virulent poison on the child. He dug his fangs deep into all the limbs of the little boy.' Those watching from the shore looked on with growing horror, and many, including Yasoda, fainted. But soon the Lord escaped from the serpent's

coils, leaped high into the sky and, landing on Kaliya's
outspread hoods, began to dance. The waters of the pool
lashed against the shore to provide the music and the
waves kept pace with the beat. Under the relentless
pounding of his feet, Kaliya, gravely wounded, accepted
defeat. His many wives, the nagins, begged the Lord's
forgiveness. In Vishnu Purana they pleaded with the Lord
thus:

> Thou art recognised, O, God of Gods!; thou
> art the sovereign of all . . . have mercy on us.
> [And Kaliya himself said:] O, God of Gods . . .
> Thou art the supreme, the progenitor of the
> supreme (Brahma): thou art the supreme spirit,
> and from thee the supreme spirit proceeds . . .
> It is in the nature of snakes to be savage, and I
> am born of their kind: hence this is my nature,
> not mine offence . . . Spare me my life; I ask no
> more.

And Krishna set Kaliya free but on condition that
he, his wives and entourage would leave the Yamuna
forever and reside in the ocean. The marks of the Lord's
feet on his hood would protect him there from any
further danger.

The manner in which Krishna subdues Kaliya has a
fascinating quality about it. The dance to victory, the

effortless rhythm of the Almighty's pace of creation and destruction, the ease, the grace, the sheer play in the manifestations of the Lord's will, to which wind and water provide enchanted accompaniment, are beautifully brought out in the narrative. Indeed, this is the first inkling in textual material of Krishna as 'natawara' (the dancer), an aspect that would see mesmerizing elaboration in the famous rasa dance of his later years.

A distinct cluster of incidents from Krishna's childhood brings out his superhuman physical powers. When but three months old, he is said to have overturned a loaded cart by a kick of his little legs, described in the Bhagavata Purana as 'more tender then the creeper clinging to a tree'. Not much later, Gokula was attacked by the demon Trinavarta, a servant of Kamsa. Trinavarta took the form of a blinding whirlwind and carried Krishna away. No sooner had he done so than he realized that the infant's weight kept dramatically increasing. Krishna clung so tightly to Trinavarta's throat that the demon's eyes popped out and he dropped down dead. A very popular incident is of Krishna, the toddler, dragging a heavy wooden mortar to which he had been tied by Yasoda as punishment. After it had been pulled some distance, the mortar got stuck between two arjuna trees, but such was the child's strength that they were uprooted. The trees were none other than two Gandharvas, Nalakuvara and Manigriva, who due to a curse in their previous birth, had been imprisoned in the form of trees. The Lord's touch gave them release, and the cowherds shook their heads in bewilderment at the miraculous feat of this little baby in their midst.

A host of demons, in the form of different animals, reptiles, or birds, were killed by the child Krishna and Balarama. Vatsasura, sent by Kamsa, came in the guise of a calf; Krishna recognized him, and catching him by the hind legs and tail, swung him round until he fell dead on top of a wood apple tree. Bakasura took the form of a giant crane and caught Krishna in his beak, but the Lord effortlessly ripped his beak apart as though it were a blade of grass. Aghasura, the brother of Putana, transformed himself into a huge python. Such was his size that his mouth appeared like a huge cavern, and the young gopas unsuspectingly walked in. Inside the demon's belly, Krishna miraculously increased his size; Aghasura's passage of breath was checked and he fell down dead. The asura, Arishta, in the form of a terrible bull, under whose hooves the very earth trembled, attacked Krishna, but the divine lad pushed him back eighteen feet, tossed him to the ground, and wrenching out one of his horns, battered him to death with it. Kesin, another dreadful asura sent by Kamsa, came in the form of a wild horse; fire spewed from his mouth, his eyes were red like embers, his body was black, and his size and speed sent the clouds scattering. Krishna caught him by his hind legs and threw him as easily as he would a discus. Wounded but not yet dead, Kesin came charging again, but the God of Gods stuck his fist into his mouth and choked him to death. (Hence Krishna is also called Kesava—the conqueror of Kesin.) Balarama was equally capable of such acts of valour. The ass-demon Dhenukasura infested a palm grove, preventing the gopas from eating the fruit. Fearless Balarama caught hold of the dreaded demon by his hind legs and whirled him around till he fell dead on top of the trees.

These tales of valour must have been based on real-life incidents of a heroic figure. The nomadic-pastoral community subsisted at the edge of thick and dense forests in which wild beasts abounded. Feats of courage and bravery in encountering such animals were probably in due course woven into folklore, which, by the time of the Puranas, coalesced into material for the Krishna legend. The historical Krishna must have himself been such a figure. From the religious point of view, what is noteworthy is that his depiction in such situations is of one who remains supremely unruffled, achieving his ends without the slightest trace of effort, as though the adversary was created merely to provide him with a means to casually unfold his will. The beast could be more ferocious than anything the human mind could imagine, but Krishna, always unperturbed, dealt with the situation with a smile on his face, in flawless control, as if he were at play. Since the world itself was deemed to be a manifestation of his play, any overt act of will on his part, in however difficult a situation, could not but be an extension of that play. However, in striking contrast to the portrayal of the unmoved and unblemished Lord is the description of the destruction of his demonic victims. The Puranas excel themselves in painting the most gory accounts of their death, the blood oozing out, the limbs breaking, their frenzied threshing about in pain, and the final death convulsions.

The image of Krishna the butter thief has caught the imagination of both believers and non-believers in a way few other images have. Krishna, on all fours, holding a ball of butter in his hand (laddoo Gopal), is a ubiquitous icon all over India. It is an aspect which has found pervasive reflection in both sculpture and painting, and is a favourite theme in the folk songs, poetry and plays depicting his life. For those initiated in his lore, whether by birth, faith or exposure, the acceptance of this theme of his childhood is unquestioning, even axiomatic. For those not so initiated, it is a matter of some surprise that a god, who ought to be the very symbol of rectitude, should in fact be celebrated for his stealing. It is worthwhile, therefore, to dwell a little on this 'peculiar'

trait of the blue god.

The world, according to Hindu mythology, was created as an extension of the Almighty's leela or divine play, the effortless unfolding of his unbounded energy. In this sense, the Supreme, when incarnate in the form of a human 'avatar', merely continues that play. This leela is beyond conventional morality, but not because that is its essential character. It is beyond such categories because it emanates from Him who is goodness incarnate. Thus, the butter thief is but one more manifestation of his infinite, untainted and joyous energy. It is god merely playing a role, but with gusto. Rama, the hero of the *Ramayana*, and also an avatar of Vishnu, was known as Maryada-Purushottam (rectitude personified). In contrast, Krishna's appellation is that of Leela-Purushottam (playfulness personified). He is also regarded as being the 'purna avatar' (the complete incarnation). Krishna, the complete god, had to be, therefore, the complete child—not only good but also mischievous, not only obedient but also wayward, not only well-behaved but also troublesome. His was not a portrayal of the divine accepting the human mantle with reluctance. As the butter thief, he is the uninhibited child, wilfully pursuing his aim, oblivious to the categories of right and wrong in adult life. This boisterous conduct is expected of him, and he cannot but live up to this image. And there is to his stealing a projection of overwhelming innocence. He takes what he wants because he has not yet learnt that he is not expected to do so. He asks for what he wants and throws a tantrum if denied, because he knows no other way of getting his way. The gopis' anger at his conduct is never sustained for long. They complain to Yasoda but mostly in mock indignation. Yasoda scolds him, even punishes him, such as when she ties him to the wooden mortar, but her stern visage is perpetually on the verge of breaking down under an upsurge of maternal affection. Indeed, his mischief is so attractive in its aggressive innocence, that the gopis— quite hopelessly in love with this adorable child—miss it when he fails to raid their homes.

The cult of the 'child-god' was based upon, and grew on, the dynamic tension inherent in such an appellation. A child is particularly accessible and capable of appropriation; but the simultaneous knowledge that in reality the child is the Almighty, merely—and graciously —allowing himself to be approached in such a form, fuses the feelings of affection and love with awe and reverence.

Surdas, to whose contributions we will come a little later, was particularly adept at bringing out this dynamic tension in his poems dealing with Yasoda and Krishna.

Quoting from Kenneth E. Byrant's *Poems to the Child God*,

> The mother says 'Dance!,
> Krishna, dance and I'll give you butter!'
> His tiny feet pound and stamp upon the earth,
>   his ankle bells ring;
> Sur sings the praises of his name,
> earth and heaven resound with his fame,
> but the Lord of the Three Worlds, dances
> for his butter.

Or again,

> He whose glances frighten Time itself
> Him his mother threatens with a stick.
> He, the fear of whom drives wind and water,
>   sun and moon,
> He moves at the threat of a little stick.
> Which form pervades earth and sea,
> yet is not to be found in the Vedas
> That form you cause to dance at a snap of your
>   fingers, here in your own very yard.

The vulnerability and approachability of infancy
became the flip side of the infinite power and grandeur
of god. Several stories of Krishna's childhood play on

precisely this vibrant dualism image. Yasoda scolds Krishna for eating mud and, when he denies doing so, forces him to open his mouth. In his mouth she sees the entire universe—the stars and the planets and all the galaxies, all things animate and inanimate, even the senses and the mind. She goes into a trance but the Lord, through his power of 'maya', makes her forget this vision, and he is back again as the erring, defenceless child, feigning innocence before his angry mother. Another favourite story is of Yasoda catching Krishna stealing butter. Her patience tested beyond control, she resolves to punish him by tying him to a wooden mortar. But every time she attempts to tie the knot, the rope falls slightly short. Finally, seeing her vexed, the child-god allows her to succeed, but only to later happily crawl out, effortlessly dragging the heavy mortar behind him. There is also the story of a gopi rushing to tell Yasoda that her darling son, caught stealing butter, has been locked up by her. But her amazement knows no bounds when she sees Krishna playing about in Yasoda's home. Stunned, she rushes back to her home and finds Krishna locked up as she had left him. The child, supposedly under her control, had once again given dramatic evidence of his essential self that was beyond such control. Such evidence was usually in the form of a flash, a momentary vision, deliberately willed by him to quickly lapse into the normal relationships and situations dictated by his human role.

The recognition of such duality—child and god—could produce startling outpourings of piety. In fact, from the tenth or eleventh century to the fourteenth or fifteenth, there developed a specific genre of Tamil writing called 'pillai Tamil'—poetry of the child—which formalized into ten sections the ritual celebration of childhood. In *Krishna, the Butter Thief*, J.S. Hawley says, these ten sections were:

- Kappuparuvam—the invocation of the deities for the protection of the child;
- Cenkiraipparuvam—literally, 'wavering', as a blade of grass waves in the wind and as the head of a young child wobbles before the infant can hold it up steadily;
- Talapparuvam—cradle songs, lullabies;
- Cappanipparuvam—clapping;
- Muttapparuvam—when the child learns to kiss;
- Varanaipparuvam—summoning the child;
- Ampulipparuvam—playing with the moon;
- Cirrilparuvam—when the child builds small houses of sand or mud;
- Ciruparaipparuvam—when the child learns to beat a small drum;
- Ciruterparuvam—in which the child drags a small wagon or cart behind him.

The worship of the child Krishna with its plentitude of nuance came to the fore with Surdas' *Sursagar*, written in the sixteenth century, and Bilvamangala's *Krishnakarnamrita,* composed around AD 1300. Hitherto, the stock of incidents in the life of Krishna as a child were limited. But the works of Surdas and Bilvamangla removed all constraining parameters in the imagery elaborating the child-gold's activities. The *Sursagar* contains several hundred poems of which a substantial number are devoted to the child Krishna. The few examples given below provide an inkling of the amazing spectrum of Sur's portrayal and his deep insight into the psychology of a child's behaviour.

Krishna in the cradle

Yasoda lulling Hari to sleep,
Shaking the cradle, cuddling and fondling,
Singing to him a song.
My darling is sleepy
Why doesn't sleep come along?
Come sleep, come quickly
Kanha for you does long.
Sometimes he closes his eyes
Sometimes his lips are aflutter.
Thinking he has fallen asleep
Yasoda stops her singing.
Awake still, he's up suddenly

Enjoying Yasoda's song.
Such joy as Yasoda feels
Is unattainable to the gods.

Krishna crawling

Chuckling, Kanha came crawling,
Trying to catch his reflection
In the bejewelled courtyard of Nanda.
One moment he would stare at his shadow
Then move his hands to hold it
Chuckling in delight, two teeth showing
Again and again he would try.
Calling Nanda to come and see
Yasoda watched in joy
Then covering Sur's Lord with her 'aanchal'
She began to feed her boy.

Krishna begins to walk

Kanha walks
Two steps at a time,
Yasoda's desires see
Fulfilment sublime.
'Runuk jhunuk' sing his anklets,
A sound
So pleasing to the mind.

He sits,
But then is up immediately,
A sight difficult to describe.
All the ladies of Braj tire
Of seeing such beauty divine.

Krishna denying he stole the butter

O, mother mine, I did not eat the butter
Come dawn, with the herds,
You send me to the jungle,
O, mother mine, I did not eat the butter,
All day long with my flute in the jungles
At dusk do I return home.
But a child, younger than my friends
How could I reach up to the butter?
All the gopas are against me
On my face they wipe the butter,
You, mother, are much too innocent,
You believe all their chatter.
There is a flaw in your behaviour,
You consider me not yours,
Take your herd-stick and the blanket
I'll dance to your tune no longer.
Surdas, Yasoda then laughed,
And took the boy in her arms,
Mother mine I did not eat the butter.

Many of the child Krishna's activities spilled over into his adolescence, but with decidedly amorous overtones. His demands of milk and butter from the gopis became, as he grew older, less a childish prank and more a pretext for dalliance.

The adorable Balgopal grows up to be the precocious Kanhaiya; both were irresistible in their attractiveness, but whereas the one evoked filial affection the other provoked sexual attention. This transition is demonstrated best in the tradition of the dan leela, wherein Krishna waylays the gopis as they take the milk products for sale to Mathura and demands a 'tax' from them in the form of a gift. The discovery of sexual attraction in both Krishna and the gopis is mutual. Krishna's behaviour shows it. He is now not only seeking the butter and the milk, but in obtaining them, he is forcing physical contact with the gopis.

The gopis are initially unable to give form to this new dimension to their feelings for someone whom till the other day they fondled as a child. They ask Krishna to state clearly what he wants. If it is only their wares, he can have them, but where is the need for the 'barjori', the use of force, the attempt to physically molest them? Krishna, on his part, continues to mask the overt sexuality of his actions under the conventional demand for milk and butter. But the imagery becomes transparently overloaded with double entendre. When he says that he wants to 'taste' a gopi's wares, the connotation is entirely different from the guileless context of his childhood stealing. His breaking of the gopis' 'matkis'—earthenware pots containing milk products—has an equally powerful sexual imagery. The asking of milk from a woman is not that innocent when the request is made by an adolescent with a rakish look in his eye. It does not take time for the gopis to understand how the situation has changed. They still sometimes complain to Yasoda about her son's behaviour, but when Yasoda protests that he is still but a child, they smile to themselves and steal sidelong glances at his lips.

Perhaps the most famous of Krishna's adolescent pranks was the stealing of the gopis' clothes as they bathed in the river Yamuna. The gopis had gone into the water nude. Krishna, watching from a nearby kadambha tree, stealthily stole their clothes and hung them up like so many fluttering banners on the branches of the tree. Discovering the theft, the gopis hurriedly re-entered the river to hide their nakedness. They implored Krishna to return their clothes, but he insisted that they come to him for them. Shivering in the cold water, the gopis had no option but to forget their shame and come out. With one hand they tried to cover their breasts and with the other their private parts. Krishna now insisted that they raise their hands in obeisance to him before he would give the clothes. Shyly, the gopis raised one hand, the other still somehow trying to cover their exposed bodies. But Krishna said the obeisance must be performed with both hands. Only when the gopis had raised both hands and stood naked before him did he give them their clothes.

The Bhagavata describes this incident in detail. The explosive sexual tension is not underplayed, but a religious motif is granted in explication. The gopis, by entering the waters of the holy Yamuna nude, had offended the gods; their transgression had to be brought home to them. In asking them to overcome their shame and modesty, Krishna was teaching them the importance of total surrender to him, the very baring of their souls, as it were, to him. The dip in the river was itself part of a religious ritual performed by unmarried girls every year in the first month of winter in honour of the goddess Katayani, who would answer their every prayer. Needless to say, the gopis' only prayer was that they get the son of Nanda as their husband. Krishna was aware of this and appreciated the 'purity' and 'chastity' of their sentiments. When they had bashfully put their clothes on, he promised them that their prayers would not remain unanswered. 'You will spend the nights in autumn with me,' he said, and, in so doing, he freed them forever from the cycle of birth and rebirth.

Lover

E ven a cursory reading of the textual material
available on Krishna's life leaves one in no doubt
that he sported with and made love to the gopis. Here is
what the *Harivamsa* has to say:

> With a young, new moon sailing untroubled
> through the balmy autumn nights, Krishna felt
> playful and exuberant . . . sometimes, stirred
> on by pleasurable emotions, he sported with
> girls from the camp through the dark, warm
> nights. The girls ecstatically drank in his
> countenance as if it were the moon come to
> earth. With his bright arm bands and wild
> flower garlands, Krishna's glowing presence
> made all Vraja glow. Entranced by his graceful
> ways, the girl herders greeted him joyously as
> he strolled about. They pressed their full,
> swelling breasts against him, their eyes darting
> about. Eluding the restraint of mothers, fathers,
> and brothers, the pleasure drunk girls dashed
> through the night to his side. Forming a row,
> they sang praises of his deeds, each girl striving
> to outdo the others . . . Their limbs were soon
> covered with dust and dung as they struggled
> to satisfy Krishna, like excited female elephants
> topped by an aroused bull elephant. With wide
> eyes beaming with love, the deer eyed girls

thirstily drank in their lover's dark form. Then
others had their chance to find pleasure in his
arms. When he sighed with pleasure, the girls
joyously echoed his melodious sounds. Their
hair, once carefully bound and parted, lay
strewn about as they fell back fulfilled, stray
hairs caressing the nipples of their breasts.
On many a moonlit autumn night, Krishna and
the herder girls joined in these revels, amusing
themselves in delicious play.

The Vishnu Purana states:

. . . Krishna, observing the clear sky bright with
the autumnal moon, and the air perfumed with
the fragrance of the wild water-lily, in whose
buds the clustering bees were murmuring their
songs, felt inclined to join with the gopis in
sport. Accordingly he and Balarama
commenced singing sweet low strains in various
measures, such as the women loved; and they,
as soon as they heard the melody, quitted their
homes, and hastened to meet the foe of Madhu
(Krishna). One damsel gently sang an
accompaniment to his song; another attentively
listened to his melody; one calling out upon his
name, then shrunk abashed; whilst another,

more bold, and instigated by affection, pressed close to his side; one, as she sallied forth, beheld some of the seniors of the family, and dared not venture . . . Thus surrounded by the gopis, Krishna thought the lovely moonlight night of autumn propitious to the Rasa dance . . . As each of the gopis, however, attempted to keep in one place, close to the side of Krishna, the circle of the dance could not be constructed, and he therefore took each by the hand, and when their eyelids were shut, by the effects of such touch, the circle was formed. Then proceeded the dance to the music of their clashing bracelets, and songs that celebrated in suitable strains the charms of the autumnal season. Krishna sang of the moon of autumn, a mine of gentle radiance, but the nymphs repeated the praise of Krishna alone . . . When leading they followed him; when returning, they encountered him; and whether they went forward or backwards, they ever attended on his steps. Whilst frolicking thus with the gopis, they considered every instant without him a myriad of years; and, prohibited in vain by husbands, fathers, brothers, they went forth at night to sport with Krishna, the object of their affection.

The description in the *Harivamsa* is matter of fact; its brevity reinforces its sincerity. There is in its narration the glimpse of a spontaneous folk culture unburdened with the constraints of structured morality. The Vishnu Purana bases itself on the *Harivamsa* narrative, but elaborates and embellishes it, using literary flourishes and the occasional overtone of piety to depict the transparent burgeoning of passion and desire profiled in the *Harivamsa*. It also makes a much more defined and specific reference to the rasa dance. The rasa emerges as a spontaneous and joyful chorus in which movement was transparently fuelled by the *physical* attraction between Krishna and the gopis. The dance could be fatiguing, lasting the entire night and for several nights thereafter, a conduit for the release of sexual tension and a forum for its expression. It was human choreography naturally articulating a need that demanded celebration. But even at this point it is very clear that the behaviour of the gopis with their god-like beau, and his behaviour with them, was in opposition to the accepted morality of the society in which they lived. The *Harivamsa* is unambiguous in asserting that the girls *eluded the restraints* of their mothers, fathers and brothers; and the Vishnu Purana is unequivocal in noting that the gopis were *prohibited* in vain by their husbands, brothers and fathers.

On the beginnings made by the *Harivamsa* and the

Vishnu Purana, the Bhagavata Purana built a complex edifice dealing with Krishna's love games. Seeing the jasmine come to full bloom in the cool autumn nights, the Lord, the Bhagavata writes, made up his mind to commence his love play. Hearing his flute and stirred by the moonlight caressing the forest in a gentle glow, the gopis, breaking all restraints, rushed to him. Having enticed them, Krishna, paradoxically, asked the ladies to return home since adultery would not be approved of. The gopis were however adamant; they fervently professed their love for him and explained the suffering they would undergo if denied union with him. Krishna relented and on the cool sands of the banks of the Yamuna with the heady perfume of the lilies in the air, made love to them.

> By stretching out his arms and embracing them;
> by playfully caressing their hair, by pleasurably
> stroking their thighs, loosening their waist
> cloths and fondling their breasts; by engaging
> in battles with fingernails; and by playful
> derision, glances and smiles the Lord aroused
> the women of Vraja to the peak of passion, and
> made love to them.

Fulfilled in their desires, the gopis begin to look upon themselves as superior; conceit and pride enter their feelings, and to remove these Krishna suddenly disappears from their midst, leaving them utterly distraught. Their suffering is so acute that they lose all sense of their person or surroundings. In their agony some of them begin to imitate Krishna. Others, almost insane from the pangs of separation, begin to search for him in the forest, singing in high pitched voices songs in his praise, and asking the bees and plants, the creepers and animals, of his whereabouts.

At this point Krishna reappears in their midst and starts the rasa. The Bhagavata Purana introduced a new element in the dance performance. According to the Vishnu Purana, Krishna, through his touch, created the impression in the minds of the gopis that each them was holding his hand. The Bhagavata states that Krishna actually physically multiplied himself, putting one of his arms round the neck of each gopi, so that for sixteen gopis there were eight Krishnas. Each gopi thus had Krishna for herself, and together they danced the rasa with vigour and passion. During the dance their breast cloths and the knots of the girdles and braids came loose, but in their fervour they cared not, 'delighted by the touches of Krishna'. The Bhagavata describes the finale of the love play thus:

After multiplying Himself so that there were as many forms of Him as there were cowherd-women, His Blessed Lord made love with these gopis—even though His delight is in Himself, playfully—as a game.

The gopis were exhausted by this excess of love play, and He, compassionate, wiped their faces lovingly . . . with His most blessed hand.

The gopis . . . honouring their virile lover, sang in praise of the sacred works He had done, filled with joy by the touch of His fingernails.

Vibrantly erotic, Bhagavata, like the *Harivamsa* and the Vishnu Purana, makes it clear that the gopis' liaison with Krishna was in the case of the unmarried ones, illicit, and in the case of the married ones, adulterous. The love play was also carried on in explicit defiance of the prevailing norms and code of morality. But the Bhagavata, written around the tenth century AD, reflects the cumulative legacy of several centuries of legitimizing desire and eroticism as a strand of Hindu outlook and tradition. Krishna, the lover, was the ultimate rasik—he who knows of rasa, is immersed in it and can arouse it in others.

When Krishna, sweetness and grace itself, played the flute its impact was bewitching. Indeed, his flute, with its obvious phallic connotations, was but an extension of his beauty. The Bhagavata narrates how, on hearing the melody of his flute, the gopis left whatever they were doing and throwing all restraint and caution to the winds rushed to his side as if in a trance. When the strains of his flute wafted through Vrindavan, all things became intoxicated with passion. Not even the wives of gods could resist its call. It was as if all of creation for a moment stopped to listen rapt in attention. As he played, clouds bent low to come closer to him, plants and creepers swayed in silent salute, the reeds from which his flute was made wept tears of joy, and rivers slowed their pace in involuntary obeisance. Vallabhacharya (AD 1479–1531), the learned saint and founder of the Vaishnava Vallabha sect, has categorized the sound of Krishna's flute into five kinds: when the Lord played with his flute to the left, passion awoke in women; when his face was to the right, desire surged in both men and women; when his face pointed upwards, kaama infused the gods; when downwards, animals and birds became its prey; and when he played straight ahead, even insentient things could not insulate themselves from its effect.

But Krishna's physical appeal, his madhurya, and the call of his flute were also linked to the overall ambience of the *moment* and the *setting,* moved by which alone he would set forth to evoke the erotic mood. The flute rang out most clear and compellingly with the onset of autumn, when the monsoon had spent itself, the landscape was green and lush, jasmine and coral flowers and water lilies were in bloom, and the nights were clear and full of stars. The *Harivamsa,* the Vishnu Purana and the Bhagavata categorically link Krishna's love play with the autumnal turn of season when man and nature alike were open to the seduction of Kaamadeva as never before.

In the *Harivamsa,* Krishna himself lyrically describes the beauty of autumn, and brings out forcefully why his flute could now succeed so eminently in overwhelming the shores of restraint around the brimful pool of desire. In this season, he says, the forests are thick with foliage and fruits. Flowers—the red bandhujiva, the yellow asama and the purple kovidava—are in bloom. The skies are clear, the breeze is calm, and the earth washed and clean. Rivers, no longer in spate, flow placidly, their gurgle akin to a woman's laughter. Flowering vines decorate the banks of the Yamuna. Lakes, ponds and reservoirs are full, and lilies and lotuses bloom in them like so many stars in the night. The fields are awash with the pastel shades of ripening rice. Birds—geese, cranes and curlews—dot the landscape. Cows are well fed and rich in milk, and bulls twice as lusty. There is contentment in the hearts of people, when autumn, like a beautiful damsel, strolls along the countryside.

Krishna's love play with the gopis was thus one in which the physical was interwoven with melody, grace, madhurya, a sense of moment and the resplendence of

nature. Sringara rasa was the outcome of this heady
mix. Vallabhacharya makes one of his most perceptive
comments in *Subhodhini,* his commentary on the
Bhagavata, when he says that 'in so far as a person does
not subordinate himself to the dominant mood to that
extent he lacks aesthetic taste' (from the translation in
James D. Redington's *Vallabhacharya on the Love
Games of Krishna*). This and not the half-hearted
attempts at 'moral' reconciliation best captures the
essence of the Bhagavata. Indeed, Vallabhacharya goes
so far as to say that the male relatives of the gopis—
fathers, brothers, husbands, sons—in attempting to
restrain the gopis 'were insensitive to the proper mood
of the ultimate reward, *since their sole preoccupation
was with the means'*. In contrast, the gopis, overcome
by sringara rasa, were rightly unable to control
themselves. Vallabhacharya gives the example of a boat
being carried away in a raging flood that would not
stop merely by someone shouting at it to do so. The
gopis were similarly beyond moral categories. Without
physical union with Krishna, they were in genuine
suffering; Krishna, for them, was the destroyer of
suffering (artihan) and the destroyer of anxieties
(adihan). Making love with him gave them sukha (bliss),
joy, and it is at this point that ideologically the carnal
and the spiritual make a surprising fusion. According
to the Upanishads, creation itself was suffused with

sukha and joy as both a reflection and an attribute of
the Infinite. The Chandogya Upanishad says: 'where
there is joy there is creation. Where there is no joy there
is no creation: know the nature of joy.' And in the
Taittiriya Upanishad, the seeker of truth finally
understands the mystery of Brahma: 'And then he saw
that Brahma was joy: for from joy all beings have come,
by joy they all live, and onto joy they all return.' This
ananda, this joy, was also the leitmotif of the gopis'
love play with Krishna. *The rasa leela affirmed the sexual
as a window to the divine.*

The gopis became jivatmas (individual souls) seeking
merger with the paramatma (the absolute). Physical
passion became an aspect of bhakti (devotion). The
erotic was sanctified; the spiritual was sexualized, and
once the sacred and the profane were so bridged, all
worrying superimpositions of guilt with reference to
conventional moral standards could be discarded,
opening the floodgates for the fullest 'humanization' of
Krishna, the lover. The imagination would now not rest
at seeking him only as an impersonal if accomplished
lover, available to all the gopis. He had to have a
preference. His personality was now free to be
embellished with the entire gamut of emotions in the
spectrum of love—desire, jealousy, pride, anger, remorse,
self-pity, ecstasy, union and fulfilment. His eroticism
now had unfettered social sanction. His love play could

therefore legitimately be a canvas for infinite themes, themes in which human emotion and sentiment would be uninhibited participants. Krishna, the lover, was now ready for acceptance as an absolute theme in itself. The Puranic lover was ready to be replaced by the myriad nuances of the romantic hero.

The Sanskrit classic, *Gitagovinda* (Songs of Govinda) written by Jayadeva in the twelfth century AD, became a powerfully evocative landmark in this process. Jayadeva was the court-poet of King Lakshmanasena (AD 1179–1205) of Bengal. Born in a Brahmin family, he was in early life an ascetic. But, marriage to Padmavati, a dancing girl in the temple of Lord Jagannath (another name for Krishna) of Puri, transmuted the ascetic into a wonderfully lyrical exponent of the relevance of human love. Apart from its intrinsic literary merit which is of an exceptionally high order, the *Gitagovinda* is of special importance for its path-breaking deification of Radha, Krishna's consort. Radha finds no mention in the *Mahabharata* and the *Harivamsa,* or in the Vishnu Purana and the Bhagavata Purana. The Bhagavata does mention one gopi who appeared to have temporarily won special attention from Krishna, but she is not mentioned by name and later efforts by Vaishnava theologists to derive the name Radha from 'aradhita'—the term used for the gopi in the Bhagavata—are hardly convincing. Starting

from the second century AD, Radha does find mention
in one or two Prakrit texts. The most notable of these is
the *Satasai* of Hala, variously dated to a period between
the first to seventh century AD. In Sanskrit literature,
she is mentioned for the first time in the inscriptions of
the Paramara king, Vakpati Munja of Malwa (AD 973–
94). In Tamil Aalvaar poetry there is the mention of
Pinnai or Nappinai as the wife of Krishna, but there is
not enough ground to postulate that she was the same
as Radha, or even that this lady was the inspiration for
the scattered references to a Radha in Prakrit and
Sanskrit literature.

The truth appears to be that Jayadeva intentionally
elevated Radha from a somewhat obscure, even
peripheral, personage to a central deity of worship. In
doing so he was making a conscious break with the past.
The author of the Bhagavata must also have known of
the existence in earlier literature of Radha. But the
intention in the Bhagavata was to portray the *non-
exclusivity* of Krishna's erotic energy. Its theological
imperative was solely to essay Krishna's love play as an
aspect of his divinity. Jayadeva's purpose went beyond.
He wanted to create an appropriate foil for Krishna's
erotic personality. His aim was to give to his love play
the dramatic content of a duet, in which Krishna's
passion would have an individual focus worthy of its
intensity. His goal was to bring the rasa leela down from

its pedestal of powerful but diffused intent to a stage where all the emotional props were drawn from an emphatically human idiom. Thus, Jayadeva's Radha had to be created. If Krishna was Sringaramurtimam, Radha, the object of his love, had to be Raseshvari—the very goddess of that mood. If Krishna was the God of Love, Radha had to be Rati (Rati is also the wife of Kaamadeva in Hindu mythology), passion personified. Krishna could not be portrayed as cosmically aloof. He had to be portrayed as symbolizing, in the tradition of Hindu mythology, the cosmic unity of purusha and prakriti. Together with his consort, Krishna was complete. Alone he was devoid of rasa (nirasa). Each was the object of the other's love. And both were the subject of each other's passion.

In the *Gitagovinda,* Jayadeva succeeded eminently in his purpose. Indeed, the profile of Radha as Raseshvari emerged so strongly that Jayadeva appears to have been daunted by his own effort. Stories of Jayadeva's life recount that the poet was hesitant to complete his work, afraid that he had gone too far in the portrayal of Krishna abashed at the bower of Radha. One day, so the story goes, Jayadeva had gone to the river for his bath, when Krishna, assuming his form, completed the last couplet of the work and ate the food prepared by Padmavati. When Jayadeva discovered the stanza completed and his food eaten, he interpreted it as divine sanction for the content of his work. This little story is interesting in reinforcing the point made earlier that Jayadeva's exaltation of Radha was in such measure a new step that it *needed* the projection of divine approval to ensure acceptability in the audience of that time.

The story of the *Gitagovinda* is both simple and complex. It is simple because the essential plot is structured, as in the rasa leela of the Bhagavata, on the unitary theme of separation (vipralambhasringara) and union (sambhogsringara) of love. The theme is complex because of the qualitatively new emotions it unleashes. The joy of union with Krishna and the unbearable pangs of separation from him—the story of the Bhagavata— are subsumed in a startling array of sentiments that accompany the amplification of this theme. Krishna is no longer the detached lover, reciprocating the passion of the gopis with consummate equanimity. He suffers and agonizes like Radha, who emerges as the unquestioned central concern of his amours. Her portrayal goes far beyond the plaintive, desire-besotted gopis of the Bhagavata. The new heroine in Krishna's life is a strikingly compelling woman: beautiful, aloof, proud, sensitive, brooding, wilful and passionate.

The *Gitagovinda* begins with Nandalal, Krishna's foster-father, asking Radha to take Krishna home since night was falling and dark clouds were threatening the sky. Radha obeys, but on the way home disappears into a thicket of trees with her ward, and the two make love. The secret, illicit character of the relationship is established ab initio. Jayadeva's Radha is not Krishna's wife. According to tradition—probably oral and textually scattered—but of which Jayadeva was aware, Radha was several years older than Krishna. She was the daughter of Vrishbhanu, a clan chief like Nandalal, and belonged to Barsana, a settlement not far from Gokula. The residents of Barsana migrated to Vrindavan before those of Gokula. On the way to Vrindavan, they passed Gokula, and it was then that Radha first saw Krishna. He was but a toddler then; Radha, a young girl, took him into her arms as a mother would her child. The Oedipal undercurrent in the Radha–Krishna liaison is plausible. The concept of the Mother-Goddess existed in India since prehistoric times and had been assimilated into Hindu mythology. In several sects the devi, or goddess, was not merely the consort of a male god but a supreme power in her own right, pursuing her own purpose and nurturing her followers in a protective and possessive manner. Perhaps it was the echo of such a tradition that prompted the necessity to give Radha at one level a mother-image vis-a-vis Krishna. The concept of purusha and prakriti could also provide a metaphysical explanation for Radha's greater years. According to the Samkhya-Yoga school of Indian philosophy, all of creation consists of purusha and prakriti. Prakriti is the all-embracing material substratum of things. Purusha is sentience personified. Prakriti, which has always existed, remains in a state of dissolution (pralaya) until the mere presence of purusha (purusha-samnidhi) disturbs the state of its latent equilibrium, and evolution (sarga) is set in motion. For evolutionary activity, therefore, the presence of purusha is crucial, but prakriti in its state of dissolution exists even without it. Radha, the cosmic symbol of prakriti, had thus to exist prior to the arrival of Krishna, purusha incarnate.

Radha was supposedly betrothed to one Ayana (or Rayana) while still a child. Ayana, who was much older than her, is said to have been the brother of Yasoda, Krishna's foster-mother. On marriage, Radha would be Krishna's aunt. In some accounts, Radha is already married to Ayana when she meets Krishna, and this adds a somewhat surprisingly incestuous dimension to the relationship.

The tradition has had a not insignificant following and has persisted over the centuries. One example is the highly sensitive writings of Muddupalani (1730–90), a courtesan in the court of the Nayaka kings of Thanjavur. In *Radhika Santwanam*, a Telugu text consisting of 584 poems, she describes Radha as Krishna's aunt. Krishna is to marry Ila Devi, a girl brought up by Radha, and Radha even advises Krishna on how to behave with her on the wedding night.

Given the seminal importance of the *Gitagovinda* in the evolution of the Krishna cult, it is useful to dwell on it a little longer. After their night of love in the thicket on that darkening eve, Krishna deserts Radha, and she, delirious in separation, imagines a love tryst with him.

Krishna soon abandons the other cowherd girls, and is deeply remorseful. He asks for forgiveness but Radha is unrelenting. She in her agony imagines how another woman must have made love to Krishna. (Extracts from the *Gitagovinda* unless otherwise indicated are from the excellent translation by Durgadas Mukhopadhyay, *In Praise of Krishna*.)

> Dressed suitably for the sport of love
> her hair loosened
> with flowers disarrayed,
> some other woman excelling me in charm
> revels with the enemy of Madhu . . .
>
> She looks at her lover
> and blushes with a smile.
> She murmurs softly
> in all the many ways of love
> lost in its bliss.

Her body shudders and trembles
Her passion blossoms
with sighs and eyes closing.

Krishna appears abashed before Radha but she
taunts him angrily.

Your drowsy red eyes
for being awake through the night
betray the intensity of passion
that you cherish for that other woman.

Alas! Alas! Go Madhava! Go Kesava! leave me!
Do not try to deceive me with your artful words.
Go after her, you lotus-eyed one
she who soothes your grief.

Krishna now uses a combination of remorse and
flattery to break Radha's pride. He praises her moon-
like face and the nectar of her lips, describes her as the
very ornament of his life, professes that only she can
arouse passion in him, and assures her that a rival to
her has no place in his life.

O anxious one,
abandon fear, imagining
me devoted to other women,

You alone entirely occupy my heart
with your voluptuous breasts and hips.
None other than the god of love—
the bodiless one, is blessed
to enter my heart.
O my beloved, be content in this
and allow me to embrace you.
Crush me with your hard breasts,
entwine me in your vine-like arms
bite me with your merciless teeth
inflict upon me, O beautiful one,
any punishment that you wish
and be happy.
Let my life not end
under the blows of Love
the five-arrowed one, the undignified one.

Radha's friend again urges her to meet Krishna's
mood without shame. The moment and the mood, she
says, are ripe for love. Finally, Radha relents.

So the encounter in love began,
when the shuddering of bodies
hindered firm embrace;
where the joy of contemplating one another
with searching looks
was interrupted by blinkings;

where the mutual sipping
of the honey of each other's lips
was impeded by the utterances
of small love-cries.
Yet even these seeming hindrances
enhanced the delight in love-play.

Though entwined in her arms
though crushed by the weight of her breasts
though smitten by her fingernails
though bitten on the lips by her small teeth
though overwhelmed by the thirst of her thighs
his locks seized by her hands
inebriated with the nectar of her lips
he drew immense pleasure from such sweet
    torments.
Strange indeed are the ways of love!

The *Gitagovinda* ends in a delightful mood of post-coital languidness, when, with the tension resolved, Krishna meekly obeys Radha's commands.

She said:
adorn my breasts with leaf designs of musk
put colour on my cheeks
fasten the girdle around my hips
twine my heavy braid with flowers

fix rows of bangles on my hands
and jewelled anklets on my feet.
And thus requested by Radha
Krishna who wears the yellow garment
did as she has asked him to, with pleasure.

From the fourteenth to the sixteenth centuries, a
host of poets carried forward the legacy of Jayadeva.
However, unlike Jayadeva who wrote in Sanskrit, these
poets wrote in the language spoken by the common man.
Chandidasa, who lived at the confluence of the
fourteenth and fifteenth centuries, wrote in his native
Bengali; Vidyapati (1352–1448) wrote in Maithili;
Surdas and Bihari (1595–1664) composed in Braj; and
Govindadasa, in the sixteenth century, wrote in Brajaboli.
The cumulative result was that the love lore of Krishna
and Radha moved out from the sanctum sanctorum of
the temple to the dust and din of daily life. Their erotic
love play made a transition from the refined, if
passionate, milieu of Sanskrit poetics to the earthy and
seductive medium of the lingua franca of the masses.
The Lord and his consort were removed from the rarefied
atmosphere of lotus-leaved arbours and ethereal jungle
thickets, and placed with poetic adroitness in more
familiar settings. Their rasa leela continued with
unabated ardour, but in new situations that were
inspired by the humdrum routine of ordinary people.

Two poems, the first by Govindadasa (E. Dimock, Jr. and D. Levertov, *In Praise of Krishna, Songs from the Bengali*) and the second by Vidyapati (*Love Songs of Vidyapati*, translated by D. Bhattacharya), beautifully capture the joyful turbulence of the first time Radha and Krishna make love. Radha is afraid and nervous, but that master-lover will brook no delay, and she, against her own resolve, yields to him. It is an indescribably evocative profile of the tension between a girl's diffidence and a woman's passion, the awakening of love and the losing of innocence in that sudden, pleasurable discovery of sex.

> Fingering the border of her friend's sari, nervous
>   and afraid,
> sitting tensely on the edge of Krishna's couch,
> as her friend left she too looked to go
> but in desire Krishna blocked her way.
> He was infatuated, she bewildered;
> he was clever, and she naive.
> He put out his hand to touch her; she quickly
>   pushed it away.
> He looked into her face, her eyes filled with
>   tears.
> He held her forcefully, she trembled violently
> and hid her face from his kisses behind the edge
>   of her sari.

Then she lay down, frightened, beautiful as a
    doll;
he hovered like a bee round a lotus in a painting:
Govindadasa says, Because of this,
drowned in the well of her beauty,
Krishna's lust was changed.

There was a shudder in her whispering voice.
She was shy to frame her words.
What has happened tonight to lovely Radha?
Now she consents, now she is afraid.
When asked for love, she closes up her eyes,
Eager to reach the ocean of desire.
He begs her for a kiss.
She turns her mouth away
And then, like a night lily, the moon seized her.
She felt his touch startling her girdle.
She knew her love treasure was being robbed.
With her dress she covered up her breasts.
The treasure was left uncovered.
Vidyapati wonders at the neglected bed.
Lovers are busy in each other's arms.

Desire and inhibition, passion and fear, seduction
and shame, ecstasy, and the occasional recurrence of

shame—the entire dialectic of a liaison is explored. But
the many moods of union are not always delineated in
predictable rainbow colours. The causeless hysteria and
ingenuity of lovers, their random elations and
depressions, their unfathomed joy and sorrow are also
the subject of these poets' attention. The following poem
by Chandidasa expresses some of these feelings.

> I must go.
> In spite of my kisses,
> My passionate embraces,
> He keeps repeating
> That he must go.
> He goes half a step
> And then he turns back
> With anguished eyes,
> Gazing at my face.
> Wringing my hands
> He promises returning
> He flatters me so much
> To meet me again!
> Deep is his love,
> My beloved one,
> Of such terrible passion.
> Candidasa says: then
> Rest in his heart.

The poets of this period chafed at the constraints of the hitherto accepted contours of the Krishna–Radha love games. As a genre their poetry came to be known as riti-kala or sringara-kala, wherein love, in all its aspects, was the unabashed theme. Their effort was to take the Krishna and Radha humanized by Bilvamangala and Jayadeva and depict them in as many situations as it was possible for human lovers to find themselves. It was a case of the divine imitating the human, and the human, being enriched by the divine. Like any bold man in love, their Krishna was also capable of the most daring ruses. Their Radha could dress herself up as a constable to put Krishna in her place, or steal glances at him unnoticed through a peephole in her tresses as she combed them after a bath. Some of these bards literally revelled in the novelty of a new situation. A poem by Bihari (*Bihari, The Satasai*, translated by K.P. Bahadur) goes:

> Exchanging clothes
> Radha and Krishna
> came to the rendezvous
> for love making.
> She was on top
> but dressed as a man,
> so they got the thrill
> of novelty
> even while seeming

to make love
in the normal way!

Even so, established themes—Krishna's bewitching
flute and the primeval rhythm of the rasa—were not
entirely forgotten, but the familiar invocation was often
laced with startlingly new imagery.

Chandidasa writes (E. Dimock, Jr. and D. Levertov,
In Praise of Krishna, Songs from the Bengali):

How can I describe his relentless flute,
which pulls virtuous women from their homes
and drags them by their hair to Shyam
as thirst and hunger pull the doe to the snare?
Chaste ladies forget their lords,
wise men forget their wisdom,
and clinging vines shake loose from their trees,
hearing that music.
Then how shall a simple dairy maid withstand
    its call?
Candidasa says, Kala the puppet master
leads the dance.

In the popular psyche, Krishna and Radha became
the universal symbol for the lover and the beloved.
Krishna was the ideal nayak (hero), and Radha the ideal
nayika (heroine). The use of the word ideal should not

be interpreted to mean a monotone image. On the contrary, they were the ideal precisely because their sringara-leela could accommodate a thousand variations. All lovers could not but reflect in their own personality some part (ansh) of the divine love between the two; conversely, the two incorporated in themselves the personality of all lovers. The canvas of their love was seamless, a painting which amplified and mutated itself in a myriad reflections. For this reason, but also as a facade for the expression of human prurience, an invocation of their name became a password to sanction the description of all contact between the sexes.

The meteoric growth in the stature of Radha in Krishna lore was in large measure due to the fact that Krishna was a god specially made for women. Radha acquired pivotal importance because through her feeling and personality she articulated the silent yearnings and fantasies of Indian women as a whole. Around the tenth century AD, women in India lived in considerably repressed conditions. Wifely chastity was an overpowering ideal in an unrepentantly polygamous society. Men could have more than one wife and several mistresses; women could at best strive to retain the attention of their husband. For men dalliance outside marriage had social tolerance if not acceptance; a woman was bounded by the four walls of her husband's home and even the thought of a romantic foray beyond them was unthinkable. To make matters worse, husbands were often away for long periods. An entire genre of very stirring verse—Baramaasa—came up dealing with a wife's anguish at the many seasons of the year drifting barrenly by in the absence of her husband. Widowhood was a curse, remarriage was taboo, and the plight of child-widows pitiable. Sexual frustration was thus rampant under the respectable edifice of 'stable' homes and chaste wives.

In Radha, Indian women found a symbol for the vicarious release of their repressed personalities. Radha's intense yearning for Krishna echoed their own subconscious frustrations. Her uninhibited pursuit of physical fulfilment with him mirrored their own libidinal stirrings. The secretive, illicit and adulterous nature of her affair with Krishna provided a particularly apt framework for them to identify with. Radha, the furtive rebel, determined to clandestinely break the stranglehold of social norms and customs, became an image they could readily internalize.

If Radha was the inspiration, Krishna was the object of the Indian woman's fantasy. Unlike other gods in the Hindu pantheon, Krishna's personality had a softness to it that made it conspicuously responsive to the longings and desires of women. As a child, his impish adorability tugged at the maternal instincts of the women of Braj. As an adolescent, his aggressive behaviour with

its transparent sexual overtones was secretly understood
by them. As a lover, he was prepared to overcome his
own initial scruples to respond with equal passion to
their overtures. When he danced the rasa he took care
to perpetuate the illusion that he was available
exclusively for each one of them. In lovemaking, he was
both untiring and accomplished. Above all, he was
human, treating women not just as sex objects, but
suffering like them in separation and longing. In his
company, they could relax the code of conduct imposed
by an overwhelmingly male-dominated society. They
would assume a stance of familiarity, calling him a thief,
a liar, cheat and so on—something they could never do
with their husbands. Krishna allowed women to play
out the fantasy of being in control, of being able to bend
the will of men to their commands. In the *Gitagovinda*,
Radha compelled Krishna to repent and, when they
made love, Radha took the man's position of being on
top. After they had made love, she commanded him to
plait her hair and attend to her toiletries. Mana or the
pride between lovers became, with Krishna, a two-way
street. If he on occasion had to be cajoled out of a sulk,
he too was prepared to make the effort to persuade his
beloved to relent. The *Rasikapriya,* Keshav Das's (1555–
1671) celebrated treatise on erotica, describes how
Krishna would arrange to send to an angry Radha
flowers 'longing to become fragrant by a touch of her

breasts', or an ivory necklace, yearning to fulfil its destiny by going on a pilgrimage to her bosom, 'the seat of holiness' (in M.S. Randhawa's *Kangra Paintings on Love*).

Even in its post-Vrindavan phase, the Krishna myth retained its special porousness to the sensitivities of the opposite sex. Soon after his arrival in Mathura, Krishna found time, in spite of his preoccupations with the looming battle with Kamsa, to have a liaison with Kubja, a deformed and hunch-backed woman, whom he miraculously restored to her original beauty. According to the Bhagavata Purana, Krishna knew of Kubja's secret longing for him. He therefore visited her house. 'She offered seats covered with costly silks to [him]—they sat for a while and Krishna looked at her who was feeling shy even to look at him. He knew how much she wanted him and according to his promise, he took her by the hand and led her to the inner chambers, and pleased her.'

Rukmini, the lovely daughter of the king of Kundalpur, was secretly in love with Krishna, having heard of his exploits from some wandering mendicants. But she was being forcibly married off by her wicked brother Rukma to Sisupala, prince of another kingdom. Krishna, on hearing of this, boldly abducted Rukmini and made her his queen, defeating Rukma and Sisupala in battle. In the course of several colourful adventures, he acquired more wives, the more notable among them being Jambhavati, Satyabhama and Kalindi. The Bhagavata Purana erred a trifle towards the excessive when it recounted that Krishna, defeating the demon king Naraka, rescued 16,000 virgins enslaved by him and married them all. The Bhagavata maintained however that he bestowed equal love on all his queens, ever responsive to their every wish. When Satyabhama wished to have the Kalpavriksha, the heavenly wishing tree owned by Indra himself, Krishna promptly set out to obtain it; when Indra refused to part with it, he took it away forcibly. Such was his legendary prowess in keeping all his wives satisfied and pleased that the sage Narada, so the Bhagavata says, once went to see for himself how Krishna managed it all. He was stunned to see that Krishna was individually and simultaneously available to all his wives.

The cumulative myth sustained one basic point: for women, Krishna was a personal god, always accessible and unfailingly responsive. This was in stark contrast with the real world where their husbands were shared disproportionately by the larger joint family, were hierarchically remote and, more often than not, found an outlet for romance outside the home. Krishna was the avenue to bridge this great hiatus between reality and fantasy in the Indian woman's life. He seemed to tell them that he understood their deep-seated desires;

and to reassure them that though their behaviour might seem an aberration by conventional standards, these standards did not apply to him. He gave them the 'permission for joy'. He was theirs to be moulded for whatever fantasy they wanted. He urged them—as the incident of stealing the clothes of the gopis demonstrated—to shed their inhibitions in his presence. He stood for the promise of passion and romance in their otherwise staid social world; equally importantly, and this is where complex psychological elements enter, he was prepared to be possessed and controlled by them in a manner profoundly fulfilling, both as lover and son.

The devotional poems of the two foremost female Krishna bhaktas, Aantaal and Mirabai, are congruent at this point to the discussion. Aantaal, regarded as one of the twelve Aalvaar Vaishnava saint-poets, lived in the ninth century in Tamil Nadu. Mirabai was born in 1498. It is said that as a child she was given an image of Krishna and grew so fond of if that her mother jokingly remarked that Krishna would one day be her bridegroom.

The significant common factor in the outlook of both Aantaal and Mira was that they looked upon Krishna as their husband. Both believed that in their previous lives they were gopis in Vrindavan. Mira considered herself to be the incarnation of the gopi Lalita, mentioned in the Bhagavata Purana. They both looked upon Krishna as their lover. They both sought physical union with him. They both wrote with an intensity and passion that was spiritual and erotic simultaneously.

Aantaal has left behind two basic works. In the *Tirupaavai*, a poem of thirty stanzas, she evokes Krishna by linking him with the rainfall that produces fertility. The poem, obviously basing itself on an ancient fertility ritual, describes how young girls in the village go from house to house to wake people to join in the rites. The girls go also to the house of Nanda and Yasoda, where Krishna is still asleep with his chest resting on wife Pinnai's breasts. When Krishna comes out to meet them, they tell him frankly that all that they want is that he accept them as his slave girls. ·

The desire to be 'possessed', to be 'taken over', physically and otherwise, is a recurring theme in Aantaal's verse. Her second and longer work, *Nachiyar Tirumoli*, is much more explicitly sensuous. Her burning desire for physical contact with Krishna is the most dominant theme here. In a dream she sees herself being married to Vishnu, but Krishna remains elusive. Desperate, she seeks Kaama's help in fulfilling her desires. From the days of her youth her growing breasts have been dedicated, she exclaims, only to Krishna. She entreats Kaama: 'Can't you grant me this greatest honour on earth: that with his sacred hands he touches my soft large breasts and my splendid abdomen.' The imagery of 'penetration', and often even of a desire to be violated, with its concomitant feelings of both pain and joy, is an identifiable undercurrent of her writing:

> He entered inside me and crushed me to pieces;
>   he let
> my life escape and enjoys seeing me dance [in
>   agony].
> My bones are melting, my eyes find no sleep
> for many days. I am whirling, and drown
> in the sea of suffering without the boat, the
> Lord of Venkata.
>
> I have lost the beauty of my breasts and my
> red lips, since Hrishikesha violated me.
> In the sole desire to unite with him my breasts
>   grew large
> and jumped in joy. Now
> they make my life melt away and cause
> such agony.

Mira's songs (collectively known as her *Padavali*), are perhaps less voluptuous, but no less intense. They profile a highly intimate and personal world in which nothing seems to exist except Krishna, the object of her desire.

The viraha of the gopis on Krishna's departure from
Vrindavan for Mathura falls in a qualitatively separate
category. This was not the stereotyped, temporary
separation of lovers so popular with Sanskrit dramatists
and rhetoricians. It was not even the viraha of the rasa
leela, described in the Bhagavata, where separation was
but a brief interlude in the mainstream towards a
climactic union. In this viraha, the sequence of events
unfolding in conventional love was reversed: union did
not follow viraha, but viraha followed union. And this
viraha was the final viraha, for Krishna never came back
to Vrindavan again.

At first glance, this twist to the love of Krishna and
Radha, and Krishna and the gopis, is difficult to explain.
Krishna had to leave Vrindavan for Mathura to fulfil
his mission of deposing and killing his wicked uncle,
Kamsa. Having done that he could have plausibly
returned to Vrindavan. Even if affairs of state prevented
him from living anymore in Vrindavan, he could have
continued to visit Vrindavan. After all, Mathura was
but a few miles away. In autumn, when the jasmine and
wild water lilies blossomed, and the stars shone
resplendently in the clear night sky, he could have come
again to enact the rasa. He was not unaware of the grief
and suffering of the gopis and, above all, of Radha, the

subject of his most passionate attachment. There was also the attraction of Nanda and Yasoda, and all his childhood friends. By all accounts, his farewell to Vrindavan was more than poignant. The Bhagavata describes the scene of that early morning when Krishna and Balarama, along with Akrura, Kamsa's messenger sent to summon them, drove away in their chariot for Mathura.

> Early in the morning one of the gopis got up to sprinkle water at her doorstep and to paint pictures with flour as was the custom. She saw a strange chariot at the door of Nanda's house. Dropping her vessel full of water and the dish containing rice flour she rushed to the other houses and spread the news . . . One bolder than the others went nearer and from somewhere near the house saw what was going on. She rushed out in panic and said: 'Stop that chariot! Take it away! Hide it! Do something with it!' . . . The gopis saw Krishna and he rushed to them. He was embraced by each and every one of them and they could not talk, any of them. They did not ask where he was going. They knew that he was going: it did not matter where . . . They turned to Akrura and spoke harsh words to him: 'How dare you take away

our darling Krishna with you? . . . You are
Yama, the god of death and you have come to
take away our lives. We will die if Krishna leaves
us.' Krishna pacified them and told them that
he had to go [but] . . . none of these words
could comfort the lamenting women . . . Krishna
left them and went to his playmates. They were
numb with the thought that their Krishna, their
playmate, their companion from childhood was
going to the city . . . Krishna took leave of them
and his eyes were sad since he knew he would
never come back to Vrindavan: never again to
the slopes of Goverdhan: never again to the
banks of the Yamuna. Never more would he
make sweet music on the sands when the moon
shed its soft beams: never again would he hold
the stick of bamboo in his hand and drive the
cows to the forests. He had bade farewell to his
cows. But once again he went into the sheds
where his beloved cows were standing and they
were all weeping. He wiped their tears and with
his forearm wiped his own tears and went to
the presence of his mother. He fell at her feet
and once again took leave of her. She clung to
him and he had to disentangle himself from her
restraining hands . . . After a few stunned
moments the gopis realized that their Krishna

had begun his journey to the city . . . They tried
in vain to stop the chariot. Akrura laid his whip
across the horses' flanks and at once they began
to move. The gopis and the young boys set up
such a wail that the very skies resounded with
their piteous cry . . . They stood staring in the
direction where the chariot was fast
disappearing. They wiped their eyes and stared
intently until the dust rising from the progress
of the chariot had settled down and they saw
nothing there far away in the distance. Krishna
had gone away from them.

Krishna had himself initiated and encouraged the
love of the gopis for him. His affair with Radha was
one in which he was completely and equally involved.
Why then was his departure from Vrindavan so final
and irrevocable? Certainly such a course of action would
not be attributed to whimsy or coincidence. It could
appear that his sojourn in Vrindavan, and his conscious
and definitive departure from it, was meant to convey
the one integrated message: Kaama has validity, but not
exclusive validity; sex is a window to the divine, but
not the only window; the physical is joyous, but so can
the non-physical be.

This Hindu view of life was always informed by
two parallel themes: one emphasized the legitimacy of

desire, the other stressed the joys of transcending such desire. Shiva gambolled in sexual play with Parvati for such an extended period that the gods themselves began to worry; but the same Shiva remained for years immersed in the most sublime meditation, totally oblivious to the senses. The dialectics of mainstream Hinduism were not either-or. It was not that one path was right, and the other wrong. Both were valid, for the essential premise was that there was more than one avenue to experience the bliss of the infinite. Mythology became a tool to correct the exclusivity of one approach. When Shiva, angry at being disturbed in his meditation, destroyed Kaamadeva, the God of Love, he was forced to recreate him. The empirical observation of life reinforced such an eclectic outlook. It was apparent that more than one strand combined to produce the final weave of existence, and more than one colour the complete picture of reality. In the unfolding life of an individual there was a plurality of phases, each with a dominant pursuit and emotion, valid for that particular phase, but not valid in the same manner for all of them. In the Hindu scheme of things, the ideal life had four stages (ashramas): brahmacharya, the period of discipline, dedicated to the acquisition of knowledge; grahastya, the period of the householder and worldly pursuits; vanaprastha, the period of preparing oneself to withdraw from the worldly senses; and sanyasa, the

period of the hermit, withdrawn from the material
world. This was an attempt to construct the rhythm of
life, taking into account its inevitable evolutionary
mutations. The mosaic of life was multifaceted, its
murals of many levels. Spring and autumn were
beautiful, but each gave way to summer and winter,
which had their own compensations. The day could be
resplendent, but it was inevitably followed by night, and
if the night was unhappy, it would as surely be followed
by dawn. Orgasms, however ecstatic, could not be
stretched forever. The sexual urge, however legitimate,
could not be sustained in permanence. The body,
however beautiful, could not remain untainted by the
vicissitudes of age. And desire and passion, however
intense, could not forever retain the same efficacy of
expression and fulfilment.

Krishna left Vrindavan to demonstrate this verity.
In doing so he demonstrated too the essential nature of
his own being. His involvement in Vrindavan was but
an enactment of his leela. He was a participant in the
rasa and in the escapades on the banks of the Yamuna
with Radha and the gopis, but this participation was
inherently transcendent. He was involved but it did not
involve him. He was a yogi, above the joys of attachment
and the sorrows of separation. Vrindavan may have been
possessed by him, but he could never be possessed by
Vrindavan. His rasa leelas may have proceeded for nights

on end, but at another level, he was the eternal celibate, untainted by his actions, and above its consequences.

The plight of the gopis was different. Their attachment to Krishna was real. The joy they derived in the rasa was overwhelming. Their horizons were limited to Krishna and the groves of Vrindavan and the sandy banks of the Yamuna. It was essential, therefore, that they learnt to give to their desires a form and content which went beyond the physical. Krishna's presence in Vrindavan had given sanctity to the joys of the flesh. His absence from it was meant to convey the limitations of the joys of the flesh, if pursued in isolation. Unconstrained joy was the essence of divinity. Sex was an aspect of that divine joy, but not the whole of it. The enlightened life was a balance of several goals, each rewarding only in a wholesome linkage with the other. Having revelled in the rasa, Krishna's purpose was to teach, through viraha, the possibility of achieving the same intensity of union without physical stimulus. In doing so, he was not denying the role of the senses but merely asserting that in conjunction with the pleasure of the senses, there could be pursued, as the next stage, an equally valid and certainly more autonomous (that is, less dependent on external stimuli) path to fulfilment and joy.

In the Bhagavata, Krishna explained the process to the gopis in the following way:

As for me, even when love is showered on me, sometimes I do not return it. The reason is because I want them to love me more: to become more devoted to me: to think of me and only me: to become my bhaktas. Take, for instance, a very poor man who has found wealth suddenly. If, after having it with him he loses it, his pain will be more than when he was poor, and his thoughts will be more intense about wealth: wealth which he had found only to lose it: Even so, I vanished from your sight because I wanted to know how dear I am to you and how indispensable. Your devotion to me has become more now when you went through the agony of losing me . . .

The essential logic was simple: First I give; then I take it away; then you miss what I gave; then the contemplation of what you had enables you to have without having.

The focused intensity of vision that viraha could produce was the subject of study of both erotic and rhetorical texts in India. The gopis deprived of Krishna's physical presence went through an identified phase of emotional and physical trauma. There was loss of sleep (nidrachcheda), loss of weight (tanuta), an aversion to any object not relating to the beloved (visayebhyo

vyavritti), an unconcern for shame and modesty (lajja
pranasa), delirium (unmaada) and fainting or a feeling
of senselessness (murchcha). There were other
symptoms: 'longing (abhilasha), anxiety (chinta),
remembrance (smarana), telling the qualities of the
beloved (gunakirtana), agitation and fear (udvega),
delirium and senseless chatter (pratapa), seeing all things
as consisting of the beloved (tan-maya), sickness and
fever (vyadhi, jvara), stupor or stiffness (jadata), languor
and displeasure (arati), and so forth'.

In the preliminary phase, the suffering of the
separated one—the virahini—was acute, but in time, as
a very consequence of this suffering, she achieved
salvation. The intensity of Radha's longing was so great
and the concentration of all her reflexes on the object
of desire so sustained that she became one with the object
itself. Radha, separated from Krishna, became Krishna.
She achieved oneness with him (aikya), a state of blissful
absorption in him (tanmayate). The pain of separation
vanished; sorrow and grief, longing and yearning ceased;
once rising from the ashes of their torment, Radha and
the gopis overcame the false duality between desire and
the object of desire. The obstacle of physical distance
was demolished by the over-reach of the mental vision.
And then there was the experience of a state of inner
calm and poise, suffused by bliss, a sense of fulfilment,
not entirely antithetical to the sense of joyous satiation

experienced by the same gopis in the fervour of the rasa. The gopis' joy, and the virahini's bliss was, in the ultimate analysis, akin; they symbolized two different but equally effective ways to reach the Lord; the ecstatic ardour of the gopis was contingent on Krishna's physical presence, the beatific serenity of the virahini was the end result of his absence.

The absence of Krishna did not however render him, in the eyes of the gopis, an abstraction. Their recollection of him may have acquired philosophical overtones, qualitatively different from the passion aroused in the rasa, but it was not a recollection deprived of the colour of his personality. The realization that he, as the personification of the infinite, was accessible even in his absence may have dawned, but this did not mean that his being had become attributeless, or that the appeal of his personality in the form that they knew it, had ceased to have relevance. The vision of the gopis sought to define the Lord in terms of their own experience. It was a vision that brought them into the larger arena of the basic debate in Hindu philosophy: What is the nature of the Absolute?

Surdas and Nandadas (1533–83), two luminaries of the Bhakti movement, adroitly used the viraha of the gopis to project the ideological superiority of the devotional mode of worship of a personal god. The Bhagavata had mentioned that Krishna, soon after reaching Mathura, sent Uddhava, one of his most trusted friends, to Vrindavan to console his grieving parents and the suffering gopis. Uddhava sought to fulfil this task by urging Nanda, Yasoda and the gopis not to grieve over Krishna's identifiable form as they had known it. The way to overcome this grief, Uddhava said, was by concentrating solely on the acquisition of knowledge of Krishna's metaphysical reality.

'Nanda, think on him as the Parabrahman,' Uddhava gently prodded, 'and not as your son. If you do that you will realize that he has no feelings like an ordinary man has. He is beyond the feelings. No one is dear to him and he hates no one. He has no desires and he has no likes and dislikes. He is not attached to anyone or anything. To him no one is high and neither does he consider anyone to be low. Equality and inequality do not exist for him. He has no mother: no father: no wife or children. He has no friends nor has he enemies. He is not confined by a body and so he has no birth or death.'

The gopis were sceptical. The memory of Krishna amidst them was, as yet, too overwhelming for them to accept the detached philosophical rationalization of

Uddhava. In this early phase of their viraha, their pain
had also a sharp tinge of anger at the way in which
Krishna had abandoned them. They had heard of
Krishna's liaison with Kubja in Mathura, and seeing
Uddhava, they gave full vent to their spleen.

> Lovers abandon the women they have loved like
> a veshya [prostitute] does a man who has no
> wealth: like subjects abandon the king who is
> impure: like students give up their teachers after
> they have learnt everything from them . . . like
> birds desert a tree which is stripped of its fruits:
> like guests take leave of the house where they
> have had their food: like a deer runs away from
> the forest which is burnt in a fire . . .

Absorbed in voicing their long suppressed
sentiments, they forgot the presence of Uddhava and
began to talk to a bee who was flying around. Uddhava
listened patiently to them but persisted in conveying
Krishna's central message which was the reason for his
leaving Vrindavan:

> This separation from me is good for you. It will
> make your love for me more intense. Your
> thoughts of me will become more constant and
> steady. The love for a distant object is always

greater than that one has for an object, a beloved object, which is within your reach. Please do not, even for a moment, think that I have abandoned you or that I have forgotten you. It can never be. I can never forget you and my love for you is the same as it was before, when I was with you in Vrindavan. Be comforted by my words and remember you will reach me very soon.

Surdas and Nandadas used this incident mentioned in the Bhagavata to develop a distinct genre of verse called 'Bhramargit' (Songs of [or to] the bee). The Bhramargit dealt with the dialogue between Uddhava and the gopis; however, unlike as in the Bhagavata, this dialogue becomes much more transparently a means to juxtapose two different ways of approaching the divine: the path of jnana (knowledge) as against the path of bhakti (devotion). And needless to say, in this debating match, Uddhava, the spokesman of the jnana-marg, is suitably humbled.

In the Bhramargit of Surdas, the gopis make their point with telling clarity:

Udho, hearts like ours can't change;
They're dyed with Shyam's pure blackness
    and there's no way to wash it away.

Spare us then your artful speeches
    and let's get down to the root of the matter:
The yoga you preach means no more to us
    then campa flowers do to you bees—
How could an insipid thing like that
    erase the fate that is furrowed in our hands?
Show us Shyam instead, our delight;
    one look, says Sur, and we'll come to life.

When Uddhava speaks to them of trying to attain Krishna through meditation, the gopis retort that in their viyoga (separation) they have surpassed the ascetic's concentration. When Uddhava persists with his philosophizing, the gopis are sharp in their rejoinder:

First teach yourself, you black honey bee,
    before you start teaching others.
If you had lived through it, then you'd know
    how exacting love can be.
You say your mind is still at Hari's feet,
    though you've brought your body here,
But without the living presence of his lotus eyes
    who ever has found the true way?
So stay here in Gokul! What do you care,
    since to you this world's an illusion?
This was their challenge to Udho, says Sur:
    See if there's any difference between us.

The gopi's argument had one invincible point: Uddhava was not qualified to lecture them because he had not experienced what the gopis had. Logic and rationality were beyond the purview of such a relationship. Wise counsels and learned discourses were of little avail. Philosophical dilutants could never weaken this bond. A moth, if it became aware of the folly of its action, would never go near a flame; but the fact that it did, and enjoyed doing so, pointed to the limitations of knowledge in guiding thought and action. Of what good was Uddhava's nirguna divinity, the gopis asked, when it could do nothing to assuage the virahini's pain of separation?

Warrior

Krishna's short journey from Vrindavan to Mathura was a watershed in his life. Until then his prominent characteristic was that of a carefree child and then of an accomplished lover, fulfilling his will in a pastoral setting. On reaching Mathura, he assumed the mantle of a man of the world, a dexterous player in the urbane milieu of city and state politics. This dramatic transition from cowherd to prince, from flute-player to warrior-statesman, and the equally dramatic change of canvas from the groves of Vrindavan to the decorum of kingly courts, has led some to postulate that historically there were perhaps two Krishnas, two heroic figures whose exploits coalesced in time into the image of the one Krishna that we know of today.

This line of reasoning need not be dismissed outright. Historical curiosity about the origin and evolution of deities in the Hindu tradition has led to new and authentic insights. But, in the case of Krishna, enquiries of this nature have not had—indeed cannot have—definitive answers. In spite of the sharp qualitative difference in his personality in the post-Vrindavan phase, there is much that points to the unitary aspect of his life. His mission was the elimination of evil personified in Kamsa: he came to Vrindavan to escape Kamsa, and he went to Mathura to kill Kamsa. From Mathura he sent Uddhava to Vrindavan to console his grieving parents and the gopis. The Bhagavata asserts that many years later, at Kurukshetra, on the occasion of a pilgrimage to mark the total eclipse of the sun, Krishna met Nanda and Yasoda and the gopis again. The *Mahabharata* frequently refers to Krishna as Govinda— a name that incontrovertibly associates him with his early years as a cowherd. Thus, as Alf Hiltebeitel states in 'Krishna at Mathura', 'the problem is not to find separate origins for "contradictory" aspects of a composite Krishna but to understand why his essentially unitary biography is largely split in two . . .' In Vrindavan, he is a prince in the guise of a cowherd; in Mathura and Dwarka he is a cowherd in the guise of a prince. In both, he is an avatar of Vishnu merely indulging in his effortless leela to assume many forms.

Kamsa was killed by Krishna through superior physical prowess. It was a clash of strength, in which Krishna, aided by Balarama, but without recourse to any supra-human powers, deposed and killed the tyrant. Kamsa had received due warning of the formidable strength of the two brothers. A washerman who had refused to lend them clothes appropriate for city-wear, had had his head smashed by one blow from Krishna. Kamsa's sacrificial bow, which strong men could not even bend, had been picked up by Krishna and easily broken into two. Kuvalayapida, Kamsa's massive elephant swaying in a rut, had been set upon the two young men, but Krishna had dragged it by its tail and, wrenching its tusk out, had killed the angry beast. Now there was to be a wrestling match. Kamsa's greatest wrestlers Chanura and Mustika were to fight Krishna and Balarama. The entire town had gathered to witness the match. Kamsa himself was seated in the royal pavilion. Krishna took on Chanura, and Balarama, Mustika. The professional wrestlers were full-grown men and tremendously strong, but no match for the agility and physical stamina of the two brothers. The moment to fulfil the prophecy of the death of Kamsa was now at hand. 'Like a falcon swooping down from the sky', Krishna caught hold of Kamsa, knocked off his crown, and dragged him by his hair around the arena, until he lay lifeless.

It was a dramatic moment. The people roared their approval. Kamsa's wives screamed in grief. The noise of drums rent the sky. Some skirmishing—soon quelled by Balarama—persisted. Through all of this Krishna retained his transcendental calm. Good had prevailed over evil. More importantly—unlike in many other contexts of his future life as a warrior—it had prevailed with little ambivalence. In a transparent act of daring and courage, he had demonstrated that it could prevail. Now there was other work to do. The first was to release his long-suffering parents—Vasudeva and Devaki—from prison. They had spent their lives waiting for this moment, and now that it had come, and their son, of

whose exploits they had heard so much, was in front of
them, they stood awkwardly inhibited, overawed by his
divine presence. But Krishna, always at ease in the
human realm, used his powers of 'maya' to appear before
them as nothing but their son. A tearfully joyous reunion
followed—alas much too short—for it was time also
for Nanda and Yasoda to say farewell. Their role of
custodian was over. One phase of life had come to an
end. Krishna and Balarama, so inseparable from them
thus far, had to move on to the next. This was the
inevitability of the chasm between Vrindavan and
Mathura.

Krishna reinstated his maternal grandfather,
Ugrasena, on the throne of Mathura. It was time now
for Balarama and him to prepare themselves to don the
mantle of their princely heritage. They may have
vanquished Kamsa but they were still cowherds waiting
to acquire the training of their Kshatriya lineage. As
rustic youths, so dear to the gopis, they may have
mastered the fine art of 'barjori', but to become
accomplished princes they now needed to master the
formal disciplines of logic, prosody, grammar, phonetics,
astronomy and etymology. The strength and daring of
the killer of the dreadful asura Kesin may have been
fabled; but the grandson of Ugrasena, ruler of Mathura,
needed also to know about the science of warfare and
the relative merit of all the weapons used in battle. The

gopis of Vrindavan may have been content to see a
garland of wild flowers around Govinda's neck; but the
scion of Mathura had to undergo the 'upanayana'
ceremony where a sacred thread was put on his body.
In Vrindavan, Kanha's flute was enough to give the gopis
an insight into the divine; but in Mathura, Krishna's
mind had to be given a formal grounding in the Vedas
and the Upanishads. Balarama and he spent sixty-four
days and nights in the custody of Guru Sandipani,
renowned for his learning and wisdom, and emerged
masters in all the sixty-four arts and crafts.

The Bhagavata narrates an interesting episode
during Krishna and Balarama's sojourn in Sandipani's
ashram. It was customary for disciples to pay one's guru
his fee in the form of guru dakshina. As his 'dakshina',
Sandipani asked the two brothers to rescue his son who
had been kidnapped to the kingdom of Prabhasha in
faraway Saurashtra. In an adventurous journey,
described with colour and verve in the Puranas, Krishna
and Balarama finally rescued the boy from the very
clutches of Yama, the God of Death. Shorn of
mythological additives, the incident, if it is based upon
historical memory of a real expedition of this nature, is
perhaps indicative of the first foray of Krishna outside
the Vrindavan–Mathura region, and his first contact
with the west coast of India, where he would later opt
to set up his own kingdom at Dwarka.

At Mathura, Krishna's career as a warrior began
by a decision to withdraw from the battlefield. Kamsa's
wives—Asti and Prapti—were the daughters of the
powerful ruler of Magadha, Jarasandha. Jarasandha had
sworn to avenge the widowing of his daughters and,
true to this oath, attacked Mathura as many as seventeen
times in the years following Kamsa's death. Krishna and
Balarama stoutly defended the city; the city did not fall,
but Jarasandha was not defeated either. It was an
unacceptable impasse, which was taking a heavy toll of
the people of Mathura. Then Jarasandha was joined in
his depredations by an 'outsider', Kalayavana, who
besieged the city at the head of his huge army of
'mlechchas'. It was at this time that Krishna decided
that discretion was the better part of valour. It was better
to retreat to fight another day, than to fight when defeat
was certain. Such a clinically realistic approach to
warfare was something new. It went against the grain
of the prevailing Kshatriya code of honour, which upheld
values of sacrifice and valour over those of strategy and
expediency. A Kshatriya's code was to fight. To retreat
in a fight was tantamount to betraying that immutable
code. Krishna's decision to withdraw from Mathura
must therefore have had its strong detractors in his time
from even amongst his own followers. One evidence of
this is the somewhat derisive epithet 'Ranchhor'—
relinquisher of the battlefield—that has survived to this

date in association with his name. In the town of Dwarka
he is, in at least one important temple, even worshipped
by that name—evidence, if any were needed, that over
time the overwhelming appeal of his myth made
palatable even those of his actions which were not
entirely explicable in terms of traditional expectations.

The statecraft of the decision was never in doubt.
Magadha was a powerful kingdom and Jarasandha a
formidable foe. The Bhagavata states that Krishna
deliberately allowed Jarasandha to escape on all
seventeen occasions, but this appears to be—even by
the Bhagavata's standards—a rather far-fetched
rationalization. Kalayavana was probably an invader
from across the Himalayas whose marauding hordes
could not be taken lightly. Mathura, at the head of the
Indo-Gangetic plains, was much too vulnerable a site
against such attacks. The Yadava army after the turmoil
and dislocation of Kamsa's death had little time to
recoup and consolidate. The withdrawal to the more
sheltered west coast, away from Magadha and the
northern frontiers, made sound strategic sense.
Jarasandha and Kalayavana pursued the retreating
Yadavas, but geographical distance ultimately made it
impossible for them to sustain the impact of their military
strike. Kalayavana was probably killed by cunning and
deceit rather than in open warfare. The Bhagavata says
that Krishna emerged from his fortress conspicuously

unarmed and alone, thus luring Kalayavana to pursue
him. Prof. Goswamy and Prof. Dallapiccola give an
account of the killing of Kalayavana in *Krishna, The
Divine Lover*.

> Dodging Kalayavana but leading him on at the
> same time, Krishna now entered a dark cave
> where he knew the glorious king Muchkunda
> to be asleep. Unsuspectingly, the Yavana also
> entered the cave. There he dimly perceived the
> form of a man lying asleep on the ground.
> Naturally assuming that this must be Krishna,
> he kicked him, at which Muchkunda woke with
> a start and cast on the intruder an angry glance
> which instantly reduced the Yavana to ashes.
> Muchkunda had in a bygone age, aided the gods
> against the demons and, completely overcome
> with grief, had solicited just one favour from
> them: that he be allowed to enjoy a long repose.
> 'Sleep long and soundly' the gods replied 'and
> whoever disturbs you shall be instantly burnt
> to ashes by the fire emanating from your body.'
> Krishna knew of this favour and had turned it
> skillfully to his own advantage.

The linkages between a possible historical event and
its mythological embellishment and perpetuation is once

again made evident.

The move to Dwarka symbolized the expansion of Krishna's mythic domain from the north and the east to the west of India. Dwarka was built as a fortress-city, on a mountainous perch overlooking the Arabian Sea. It was a well laid out city, and the Bhagavata speaks eloquently of its gold encrusted buildings and crystal balconies. At the heart of the city was Krishna's resplendent palace, encrusted with jewels and replete with all manner of luxuries. This was the setting of a powerful king, but as an extremely popular and poignant incident of Krishna's life demonstrates, it was power that was both accessible and human. Once a childhood friend of Krishna, by the name of Sudama, came to see him at Dwarka. Sudama was very poor and had agreed to visit Dwarka reluctantly and only at the goading of his more calculating wife. As he wended his way to Dwarka, all kinds of doubts assailed Sudama: Who would believe him when he claimed Krishna as a friend? Would the royal guards even allow him to enter the palace? Would Krishna recognize him? And if he did, what would be his reaction to see an indigent friend of so long ago? Once in Dwarka, Sudama was pleasantly surprised to find that he could enter the palace without hindrance. What is more, Krishna himself saw him approach and, even from a distance, immediately recognized him. Tears of joy began to flow down the cheeks of the ruler of Dwarka. He clasped his friend in a tight embrace and seated him on his own couch. With the greatest reverence he himself washed his friend's feet. Then he served him food with his own hands. All this while, Sudama had endeavoured to hide some handfuls of rice tied up in a rag which his wife had sent as a gift for Krishna. Sudama was ashamed of a present so wretched for a king so rich, but Krishna, seeing the little bundle, opened it eagerly and ate up the poached rice with the utmost delight. The next day, when Sudama left, Krishna accompanied him for a considerable distance to see him off. Sudama had not been able to bring himself to ask anything of Krishna. It was more than enough, he told himself, that he had managed to meet him and had been treated with so much love and respect. A huge surprise, however, awaited him when he reached home. His humble hut had been miraculously replaced by a glittering palace. Krishna had fulfilled his needs without his asking.

This little story has enduringly etched itself on the Indian psyche. Krishna's intensely human reaction on seeing his impoverished mate—a reaction that overcame the constraints of wealth and status by its sheer spontaneity—has become in the minds of the common man, a defining metaphor for the test of friendship. It has also come to be regarded as the definitive parable to emphasize the importance of human values in the

conduct of those in high office. Yesterday's cowherd
was today's monarch. Much around him had changed;
and yet, so much in him could never change. The Sudama
episode reiterated Krishna's enduring links with his past.
Sudama's journey to Dwarka, notwithstanding his initial
misgivings, so beautifully portrayed in the Bhagavata
and elaborated upon subsequently by many
accomplished writers, was meant to demonstrate the
triumph of faith over doubt.

  While Dwarka was the seat of his kingdom, the real
stage for Krishna's role as a warrior was still located
along the river Yamuna, in the familiar setting of the
north Indian plains, not far from Vrindavan and
Mathura. Krishna's aunt—Vasudeva's sister Kunti—was
married to Pandu, the ruler of the Kuru kingdom with
its capital at Hastinapur. Kunti's three sons—
Yudhishthira, Bheema and Arjuna—were thus Krishna's
cousins; this familial relationship also included in its
scope, on the same footing, Pandu's two younger sons—
the twins Nakula and Sahadeva—born from another
wife, Madri. Pandu had died early and his large kingdom
was being run by his brother, the blind Dhritarashtra.
The real power behind the throne was Duryodhana,
Dhritarashtra's unscrupulous and ambitious eldest son,
who wanted to inherit the throne and exclude completely
the five Pandava brothers from their father's legacy.
Dhritarashtra did not approve of his son's doings but

was too weak and vacillating and too overwhelmed by
love for his sons, who numbered a hundred, to stop the
machinations against the Pandavas. Duryodhana was
aided and abetted by his mother's scheming brother,
Shakuni. The most serious conspiracy hatched by uncle
and nephew was the attempt to burn alive the Pandavas
and their mother in a palace specially prepared for this
crime. The Pandavas managed to escape due to a timely
warning, but it was clear that they would no longer be
safe in Hastinapur. For some time they led an itinerant
existence dressed as Brahmins to conceal their real
identity. During their travels they visited the court of
King Dhrupad, who was conducting a swayamvara for
the marriage of his daughter Draupadi. A galaxy of
princes were gathered for the occasion but it was Arjuna
alone who could perform the feat prescribed for her
hand. Being the skilled archer he was, he shot through
the eye of a fish revolving above his head by looking
only at its reflection in a pool of water below. Krishna
was also present at the swayamvara. He had, of course,
seen through the disguise of the Pandavas, and became,
from then onwards, their closest ally and adviser.

The war between the Pandavas and the Kauravas is
the theme of the great Indian epic, the *Mahabharata*.
Krishna, ranged on the side of the Pandavas, played a
central role in its unfolding events. It is not the intention
here, nor would it be feasible, to narrate the entire

sequence of events, all the plots and sub-plots, and the scores of characters, that constitute the background to Krishna's role in the epic's narrative. It would perhaps serve our purpose if we touched upon the main events of his involvement in the great fratricidal conflict. At a generalized level, Krishna was on the side of good and against evil. The Pandavas were sinned against. The Kauravas led by Duryodhana were the villains. His participation was, therefore, for the restoration of righteousness and the defeat of adharma. However, while in broad terms this description of his role is sustainable, the fineprint of his involvement militates against the assumption of any unquestioned ethical clarity. What is profiled much more clearly is Krishna the strategist, at one moment the sober statesman, but very often also the shrewd manipulator bent upon achieving his purpose irrespective of the means employed.

The Pandavas established their own kingdom at Khandavaprastha, a region which was a half of the Kuru kingdom in extent, but barren and desolate. The territory was given to them by Dhritarashtra after he had invited them with all honours to return to Hastinapur from their volitional exile. Vidura, Dhritarashtra's younger brother, had personally journeyed to Dhrupad's court to request the Pandavas to return. The brothers were reluctant, but Krishna advised them to accept the invitation. When

Dhritarashtra made the offer of Khandavaprastha, Krishna knew that it was an unfair and unequal settlement. But again, he advised Yudhishthira to accept it. He was present at the formal ceremony arranged by Dhritarashtra to consecrate Yudhishthira as the ruler of Khandavaprastha. And finally it was he who helped the Pandavas transform Khandavaprastha into a rich and fertile region. Indraprastha, its capital, soon emerged as a city to rival all others. According to the *Mahabharata*, at Krishna's behest, Vishvakarma the celestial architect himself planned and executed the construction of the city.

Having made his kingdom secure and prosperous, Yudhishthira wanted to perform the traditional Rajasuya sacrifice to project his political pre-eminence among the other states and kingdoms. His advisers were enthusiastic, but Krishna, whose advice was as usual sought, advised caution. In a remarkable portrayal of the unsentimental, calm and dispassionate military strategist, Krishna clinically essayed the political situation. It would be a mistake, he said, to underestimate the strength of Jarasandha, the as yet unvanquished ruler of Magadha. Jarasandha's position was bolstered by a host of important alliances. Sisupala, prince of the Chedi kingdom, was a good friend of his, and other Kshatriya scions—Dantavaletra, Rukmi and Paundraka Vasudeva—were known to be close to him.

Yudhishthira's own cousin, Duryodhana, would, in a conflict, probably be on the side of the Magadha ruler. Bhishma, Dronacharya and Kripacharya, formidable warriors of the Kuru kingdom, would perforce have to support Duryodhana. Even if they did not, Karna, an archer to match Arjuna, would surely go with Duryodhana.

> 'With such a formidable team of foes you have absolutely no chance of performing the Rajasuya,' Krishna argued. 'Jarasandha has captured ninety-eight kings and he keeps them imprisoned. He has an idea of making a sacrifice of royal heads to lord Sankara. The man is mad. But he is too powerful to be ignored or to be defeated. So long as this Jarasandha is alive, your hopes of performing the Rajasuya are thin indeed. If, however, we manage to kill him, then there is nothing to worry about. The other kings, seeing him killed, will not have the courage to defy you and your brothers. This is my firm opinion. Think of a way to kill Jarasandha, and the rest is easy.'

Jarasandha was killed, but not in open battle. According to a plan hatched by Krishna, he was tricked into accepting a one to one wrestling match with

Bheema. Even in such a bout, he would not have been
defeated, for he had been gifted with divine powers by
the sage Chandrakansika. Every time Bheema tore his
body into two, the two halves would miraculously rejoin.
Bheema was at his wit's end, until Krishna came to his
rescue:

> When he was able to manage it, Krishna caught
> the eye of Bheema. Krishna had a small leaf of
> a plantain in his hand. He split the leaf into
> two. He then turned one piece round and threw
> the two pieces at two corners of the floor.
> Bheema understood what he was trying to say.
> Again, Bheema threw Jarasandha up in the air.
> He caught the descending form of the king by
> the legs. He tore him in two. Bheema now threw
> the two pieces at two corners of the hall such
> that one leg and one half of the head were
> corresponding. The halves did not join up any
> more. Jarasandha, the favoured of Shankara,
> was now dead.

With Jarasandha out of the way, Yudhishthira's
Rajasuya was eminently successful, and a grand
ceremony was arranged for his coronation. Kings and
princes and sages and distinguished guests poured in
from all the four corners. The Kauravas, led by

Duryodhana, had been specially invited. Krishna, of course, was one of the first to arrive. After the ceremony was over, it was incumbent upon Yudhishthira to express his gratitude to each of his guests personally. As per traditional practice, it was also necessary for him to identify a special guest of honour. Bhishma's advice was to select Krishna for this honour, an advice more than enthusiastically accepted by Yudhishthira and the Pandavas. Accordingly, Krishna was ritually 'worshipped' by Yudhishthira. In conformity with the custom to show respect and obeisance, Yudhishthira, aided by Sahadeva, washed Krishna's feet with his own hands. Appropriately, so the *Mahabharata* says, the very heavens rained down flowers on this happy event.

As the rift between the Pandavas and Kauravas widened, the destruction of the Pandavas became Duryodhana's sole obsession. In his uncle, Shakuni, he found an ideal tactician to achieve this goal. Together, they devised a strategy to entice Yudhishthira to a game of dice. Yudhishthira, being no match for Shakuni's mastery over the dice, predictably lost the game, on which he had staked all his material possessions, even his four brothers and wife Draupadi. Duryodhana invited all Pandavas to another game of dice. Incredibly Yudhishthira, unable to overcome the gambler's instinct, accepted. This time there was only one stake: whichever side lost would have to go into exile in the forest for thirteen years. Yudhishthira's folly reduced the Pandavas to homeless wanderers.

Once the exile was over, the Pandavas sought their kingdom back but Duryodhana refused. Krishna, who tried to make peace on behalf of the Pandavas, failed in efforts. War thus became imminent. His personal investment in trying to achieve a peaceful solution notwithstanding, Krishna was the quintessential warrior. The political setting of northern India at the time of the 'historical' Krishna, certainly provided an appropriate stage for his war-like exploits. The Aryans were in the process of colonizing the region. Small and competing kingdoms had come up along the Gangetic Valley. These were often in conflict with each other. New territory had to be won and secured. Forests had to be cleared for human settlement. Weapons of copper and bronze were being discarded by the revolutionary discovery of iron. One account, in *Krishnavatara* by K.M. Munshi, which does not claim to be a historical rendering but is nevertheless based on a thorough study of traditional texts, has these extremely interesting passages describing the discovery of iron ore by Krishna:

One night he sat watching the sacred fire

burning and crackling on the altar, when he saw, as usual, a fiery stream of copper being released by the (fire) god. As he diverted it into a narrow gully which young Garuda kept filled with water, he felt highly dissatisfied.

For long he continued to invoke the gods to send him super human arms, offering fresh fuel and coconut oil at the altar. Suddenly, his eye caught sight of something miraculous. One of the rocks, which had not melted with the others, began to glow like the sun, fiery as at mid day, golden red as at dawn. It was a strange sight. It was a sign from the gods, thought Krishna. The other rocks had already melted freely, but not this glowing, fiery ball of light and heat.

He continued to invoke the gods and to pour his offerings into the fire. The flames leapt up from the altar. A stream trickled out of the glowing ball. When diverted into the gully, it sizzled frantically, a fiery steam issuing from it. When the molten liquid became cool, Krishna picked it up and was delighted that the gods had answered his invocation. He flung it at the copper blade of the sword; the blade broke into two. He shot copper arrow-tips against it; their edges were blunted. At last Indra had sent him a piece of his thunderbolt, heavy and unbreakable.

Krishna then discovered that the little red rocks
... were the favoured offerings of the Fire God,
for when they were offered, the fiery liquid
which came from the altar became pieces of
thunderbolt.

Krishna and Garuda made a search for such
reddish rocks all over the hill. When they were
found in sufficient quantities, they were offered
to the sacrificial fire. Though the Fire God was
difficult to please, Krishna satisfied him with
copious offerings of coconut oil and sandal
wood. Then the fire blazed high. The flames
leapt up. The red rocks glowed red. A stream
of molten liquid flowed out. Cooled and
tempered, hammered and sharpened, the
thunderbolt emerged as a shining weapon—a
weapon which could easily break copper and
flint weapons. It was the gift of the gods.

The above is obviously an attempt to reconstruct
what might have been but is not entirely implausible. In
general terms there can be little doubt that the period of
the historical Krishna coincided with a phase in which
military adventurism and acts of personal valour and
bravery were the stuff from which cult figures could
easily emerge. A.L. Basham, one of the most eminent

historians of ancient Indian culture and history has, therefore, rightly surmised that '. . . it seems certain that there is some historical basis for the legend of the hero-god; but evidently tales of many heroes from many ages and many parts of India have been fused together in the Krishna myth . . .'

Given Krishna's mastery over the arts of war, both the Pandavas and the Kauravas were keen to have him on their side in the imminent battle. According to the *Mahabharata*, Arjuna journeyed to Dwarka to obtain a commitment of support from him. Hearing of this, Duryodhana also journeyed to Dwarka. Both arrived simultaneously, but it was Duryodhana who first entered Krishna's bedroom. Krishna was asleep then; waiting for him to awake, Duryodhana sat down on a chair at the head of the bed, while Arjuna deferentially took a place on the opposite side, near the feet. When Krishna awoke he first saw Arjuna, and then turned around to notice Duryodhana. Duryodhana was the first to speak. He bluntly asked Krishna to be on his side, and said that since he had arrived first, his request should get priority over Arjuna's. Krishna's answer was that while Duryodhana may have arrived first, it was Arjuna whom he had seen first on awakening. Arjuna was also younger than Duryodhana, and had, therefore, the right to ask first. The choice Krishna said was between him personally, and, his well armed and extensive Yadava army. Furthermore, whichever side he may be on, he would not fight himself. He would be weaponless, providing only unarmed support. To Duryodhana, given these options, the choice was abundantly clear. He was most relieved, therefore, when Arjuna unhesitatingly chose the non-fighting Krishna and allowed Duryodhana to have Dwarka's formidable army.

Why did Krishna not take up arms in support of the Pandavas? After all, he was fully convinced of the justness of their cause. And that being the case, why was his involvement in their support qualified? On more than one occasion he had said that the Pandavas—specially Arjuna—were closer to him than anyone else. Why then a self-imposed restraint on the degree of his participation in their struggle to obtain their rights? Perhaps the rights and wrongs in human affairs are never that categorically clear for unambiguous divine involvement on any one side. Perhaps the purpose was to demonstrate that even without arms his mere presence was more than enough to ensure victory. Or perhaps, it was a symbolic gesture, meant to convey, as in so many other aspects of his life, the perennial shadow play between his mortal form and his essential divinity. He would be a participant, but at a transcendental level. He would be involved, but in a detached manner. In his human avatar he could not remain an aloof observer. But being God, his association, however vigorous, would always be tinged by a sense of distance.

Krishna's role in the actual war is not beyond controversy. The controversy concerns the means he employed, even while not fighting himself, to ensure the victory of the Pandavas. There are at least six incidents in the *Mahabharata*, crucial to the final outcome of the war, which call into question the ethicality of his actions in terms of the prevailing code of fair play, or at least in terms of the *expectation* of fair play from him.

On the eve of the war, Krishna's attempt was to wean away the mighty warrior Karna from the Kauravas. This he did not by appealing to Karna's sense of rectitude, or by persuading him to see the legitimacy of the Pandava's claims. His strategy instead was to use a crucial nugget of information about Karna's personal life to break his pledge of unshakeable loyalty to his childhood friend and benefactor—Duryodhana. Karna was in reality the first-born of Kunti, from an unintended liaison before her marriage with Surya—the Sun God. Krishna was aware of this, and chose this moment to reveal the truth to Karna. The news had a traumatic impact on the young warrior. At one stroke the Pandavas, whom he regarded as his most implacable foes, were revealed to be his brothers. Krishna did not stop there. He went on to outline in detail the advantages that would accrue to Karna were he to betray his old loyalties:

You know that a son born to a woman when she was a maiden, becomes, by law, the son of the man she marries. Accordingly, you are a Pandava. You are the eldest of the Pandavas. You are a Pandava on your father's side. You are a Vrishni, my cousin, my relative, on your mother's side. Come with me now. I am going to Yudhishthira. Your brothers will fall at your feet. All the kings who have assembled to help the Pandavas will honour you as the eldest Pandava. You will be crowned by them as their king. You will be the king and Yudhishthira will be the Yuvaraja. He will lead the white horses of your chariot to your presence and lift you to your seat. The dark and beautiful Draupadi will belong to you, since you are a Pandava. Yudhishthira will get into the chariot after you. The mighty Bheema will hold the umbrella over your head. Your younger brother Arjuna will be your charioteer. He will hold the reins over your horses. Nakula, Sahadeva and I will be walking behind your chariot.

Krishna's mission did not succeed because Karna, in spite of the enticements somewhat blatantly outlined to him, refused to give up his friendship of Duryodhana who had stood by him when he needed support most.

But Krishna's request was not a complete failure either. Karna's emotional equipoise was shattered. His animosity to the Pandavas was weakened. His hitherto resolute morale for battle was shaken. The ground had been prepared for him to concede a boon of the greatest significance to Kunti, who met him a few days later. Kunti too was unable to persuade him to forsake Duryodhana; however, not wanting to completely disappoint his mother, he promised her that he would not attack Yudhishthira, Bheema, Nakula and Sahadeva. The duel with Arjuna was something to which he was irrevocably pledged, but, at all times, he assured Kunti, at least five of her sons would remain alive.

During the war, the Pandavas, at the explicit urging of Krishna, managed to kill the top warriors on the Kaurava side by means which were at best expedient and, at worst, deceitful and unfair. Bhishma was more than a match for any on the Pandava side. His arrows were wreaking havoc on the Pandava army. In consultation with Krishna, the Pandavas decided to meet Bhishma and ask him how he could be defeated. Even though he was duty bound to fight on the side of Dhritarashtra, Bhishma, at a personal level, had the greatest love for the Pandavas. Krishna's clear reasoning was that if Yudhishthira posed the question to Bhishma, the grand old man would certainly reveal the answer. The plan worked. 'Place the warrior Shikhandi before me,' Bhishma said, 'and I will have to put down my bow!' Bhishma had sworn never to fight against a woman, or even a man who had once been a woman. Shikhandi was a man only in appearance. In reality, he was an incarnation of princess Amba of Kashi. Amba had wanted to marry Bhishma, but, the latter, wedded to his oath of celibacy, had spurned her advances. The princess had then sworn to avenge this humiliation. Born again as Shikhandi, she led the attack on the venerable warrior. Bhishma relinquished his arms, and Arjuna's arrows were quick to pin him down.

Drona, the towering guru of the Kuru clan, was another formidable warrior whose depredations were taking a heavy toll of the Pandava forces. Krishna's plan to kill him was ingenious. It was well known that Drona was extremely fond of his son Ashwathamma. If he was told that Ashwathamma had died, Drona would, Krishna said, lose all desire to fight. But Drona would believe this news only if Yudhishthira, who never spoke an untruth, conveyed it to him. Yudhishthira baulked at being told of his role; Arjuna too was disapproving. But Krishna's exhortations were coldly persuasive. 'If Drona lives for but half a day, the Pandava army will be wiped out,' he said. In a study by R.C. Gupta, Krishna says, 'A lie to save lives is not immoral. In fact, in certain situations a lie is permissible. A lie in the presence of women, in marriages, to save cows, or to rescue a

Brahmana, is not wrong.'

The plan was implemented with Machiavellian skill. Bheema had killed an elephant called Ashwathamma. Yudhishthira, the reluctant conspirator, did not tell a complete lie when he told Drona, 'Ashwathamma is dead!', adding in an inaudible whisper, 'the elephant called Ashwathamma.' The shattered Drona, unquestioningly believing Yudhishthira, lost his will to fight. A few caustic words from Bheema on the inappropriateness of a Brahmin indulging in wanton killing were enough to make him dispiritedly put down his arms, and Dhrishtadyumna, son of Dhrupad, swiftly cut off his head.

Karna was killed when, during his fight with Arjuna, he got down from his chariot to lift its wheel sunk into the ground. It was against the rules of war to attack a man when he was unarmed, and Karna asked Arjuna to respect this code of conduct. But Krishna was quick to intervene. Fair play in war had no application, he said, to those who had scant respect for it themselves. By supporting Duryodhana's unjust cause, Karna had forfeited his right to be dealt with fairly. Eyes flaming with anger, Krishna recounted the inhuman and unscrupulous manner in which, just a few days earlier, Karna had ganged up with other Kaurava luminaries to kill Abhimanyu, Arjuna's young son. 'Kill Karna now, before he returns to his chariot,' Krishna pressed Arjuna, and the next moment, Karna, his head severed from his body, lay dead on the battlefield.

Jayadratha, the ruler of Sindhu and the son-in-law of Dhritarashtra, was killed, if not by a tampering of temporal laws, then by divine manipulation. Jayadratha had been instrumental in the death of Abhimanyu. Arjuna had sworn to either avenge his son's death by killing Jayadratha before sunset the next day, or to immolate himself. Having heard of Arjuna's oath, Jayadratha, protected by the entire might of the Kaurava army, remained effectively elusive. At the end of an exhausting day of fighting, he was still beyond the reach of Arjuna. The horizon was darkening with the imminent sunset. Krishna was worried. Jayadratha emerged triumphantly from hiding, only after he was very sure the sun had set. But just as he did so, the sun inexplicably peeped out from the darkness to shine again. This time Arjuna did not let the opportunity slip by. One arrow from his bow and the exultant Jayadratha was dead. Krishna had saved Arjuna from his vow of self-immolation by creating a false sunset to lure Jayadratha from his hideout.

Duryodhana was the last of the Kaurava brothers to be killed. With honourable magnanimity, Yudhishthira had offered him a duel with any of the Pandavas using a weapon of his choosing. Krishna was quick to chide Yudhishthira for such foolhardy generosity. Duryodhana was too good a fighter, he said, to be defeated by anybody except perhaps Bheema. Fortunately, Bheema himself challenged Duryodhana to fight him with the mace, and the latter readily accepted. The fight was long and bitter. The two opponents were evenly matched. But, after a while, it became clear that even though Bheema was the heavier of the two, Duryodhana was more agile and the better fighter. Krishna, who was watching the duel intently, confided to Arjuna that Bheema would never be able to win in a fair fight. He had to be defeated by unfair means. 'Has Bheema forgotten his vow to break Duryodhana's thighs?' Krishna asked Arjuna in a voice loud enough for Bheema to hear. Arjuna, quickly grasping Krishna's intent, smacked his own thighs as a signal to Bheema. Bheema got the message. In one forceful blow his mace smashed Duryodhana's thighs, leaving him prostrate and writhing in agony. It was against the rules of war to hit below the navel. Duryodhana was thus not expecting to be hit on his thighs. Bheema too would not have broken the rules of war but for Krishna's unambiguous urging. Balarama, who was observing the fight, was furious at the unfair means adopted. He was ready to attack Bheema, but was restrained by Krishna. Then Duryodhana, who was in his death throes, but still mentally alert, spoke. His last words were a damning indictment of the means adopted by Krishna during the war. The fallen warrior recounted each incident—the disarming of Bhishma, the killing of Drona and Karna, and, of course, the duplicitous means responsible for his own defeat. There was unconcealed contempt in his voice, and the heavens themselves seemed to endorse his stand by raining flowers on his head when he died.

Krishna's response to the accusations of Duryodhana is extremely interesting. First, he *admitted* that he had resorted to unfair means. The Kauravas, 'who were the very flowers of Kshatriya prowess', could not, he said, have been killed by fair means. The vow he had made to Draupadi at Kamyaka forest could thus be fulfilled only by the pursuit of deceitful means. Deception, Krishna said, is acceptable when the enemy is stronger. 'The gods themselves are not above it; we have only followed their example.' The Kauravas symbolized adharma. They had to be defeated. In such a situation, 'the end,' he said, 'justifies the means'. In the prevailing times, 'unsullied righteousness' could not be practised. The fourth quarter of time, the Kalyug, had begun. In this age, absolute morality would be at a discount.

The working of fate and destiny did not allow right and wrong to retain their sharply distinctive focus. 'It is the rule of time. You must not try and change the course of Destiny. She will have her way. She is unrighteous too, and she fulfils herself in many ways, mostly unrighteous.' Krishna's final argument was that in his human avatar he had to play the game as a mortal would. 'When I am living as a god, I act like a god; when my form is that of a gandharva or a naga, my actions and behaviour are in conformity with such a status; now, as one born of human parents, I must act and behave as human beings would.'

Peace and prosperity smiled upon the Pandavas after the defeat and decimation of the Kauravas. Their own sons had perished in the war, but a grandson, Parikshit, born to Uttara and Abhimanyu after the latter's death, kept the lineage preserved. This family continuity would have tragically snapped, but, as always, for Krishna's help. Parikshit had been stillborn, possibly as a result of injury to the embryo from the after effects of a special weapon launched by Aswathamma, in the last stages of the war. Krishna, true to his promise to be at hand to ensure a safe birth, miraculously resuscitated the child. In time, Parikshit grew into a handsome and responsible prince. The time for Krishna to relinquish his mortal frame was approaching. When the war had ended, Gandhari, inconsolable at the death of her hundred sons, and, furious with Krishna for not having prevented such fratricidal bloodshed, cursed him: 'You Krishna, will one day slay your kith and kin and die yourself alone in the wilderness.' Her ominous prophecy came true in a curious way. The story goes that once Shambha, a son of Krishna, along with some other Yadava boys, insulted the sages Vishvamitra, Narada and Kanwa. Shambha dressed himself as a woman and accompanied by his friends presented himself before the sages with the question: 'Will this woman bear a male or a female child?' The sages, who immediately saw through the ruse, were not amused, and cursed the boys thus: 'This woman will produce a club that will destroy the Yadava race.'

Accordingly, an iron club emerged from Shambha's belly. Ugrasena, aware of the prophecy, had the club ground to dust and scattered, but from the particles there grew fearsome iron rushes. One particle, bigger than the others, was thrown into the sea and swallowed by a fish. The fish was caught by a hunter, Jara, who, discovering the piece of iron in its belly, used it as a point for his arrow.

Meanwhile, events toward the destruction of the Yadavas were proceeding inexorably. There were evil signs and portents foretelling the imminent destruction of Dwarka. On Krishna's advice, the Yadavas left for a pilgrimage to Prabhasa. But destiny had to be fulfilled. In Prabhasa they consumed liquor and under its effect set about attacking each other. Such was their uncontrolled anger that when their weapons were expended, they used the same deadly rushes as weapons in a fight to the finish. Krishna tried unsuccessfully to stop the fighting; enraged, he himself slew several of his kin. In the end, save Krishna, Balarama and Krishna's charioteer, all the Yadavas lay dead.

In anguish, Krishna retired to the forest. Here he saw a large serpent emerge from the mouth of Balarama and take him towards the deeps of the ocean. Balarama, an avatar of Sesha, Vishnu's great serpent, had returned to his celestial origins. Krishna knew his own end was close. He despatched his charioteer to narrate the sequence of events to Ugrasena and Vasudeva. He had already ensured the survival of Uddhava by sending him on a separate pilgrimage to the mountains. Now, the emblems of his mighty power—his conch shell, mace and discus—circumambulated him and ascended heavenwards. Alone in the wilderness, Krishna sat down to meditate, one foot resting on his knee. At this moment, Jara, the hunter, mistaking the sole of Krishna's foot as belonging to a deer, shot the arrow tipped by a piece of the fatal iron club. The lethal arrow, strongly reminiscent of a similar weapon in Greek mythology, lodged itself in its target. On realizing his error, Jara fell at the Lord's feet, but Krishna, not in the least perturbed, blessed him and assured him of a place in the heavens of the gods. Then, by his own volition, Krishna relinquished his mortal frame, to became one with his essential self—eternal, unblemished and universal.

On that very day, the oceans rose in upheaval and submerged the city of Dwarka.

Saviour

When the great war was about to begin, Arjuna, the most accomplished of the Pandavas, refused to fight. The two armies were arraigned in all their military splendour opposite each other. Conches and symbols, kettledrums and trumpets sounded in the air. There was the glint of armour, as impatient warriors, legendary for their skill and valour, stood ready for battle on horse-drawn chariots and magnificently caparisoned elephants. Arjuna, standing on his great chariot yoked to milk-white stallions, asked Krishna, his sarathi (charioteer), to halt mid-way between the armies. On both sides he saw kinsmen—fathers, uncles, brothers, teachers, elders, companions. And his will faltered. He did not want to kill them. 'I desire not victory, nor kingdom, nor pleasures,' he told Krishna, 'if these are to be won at the cost of so much bloodshed.' His lips were parched, his body shook and his hair stood on end. 'It is against honour to kill one's own cousins,' he said. 'There is a special place in hell for those who destroy their family, for once the family is destroyed, unredeemable chaos is the only consequence.' And so, on the great battlefield of Kurukshetra, Arjuna, the great warrior, slumped in dejection and put his bow and arrow down, overcome by sorrow and anguish.

It is with this dramatic portrayal that the Bhagavad Gita, a text of pivotal importance in the Hindu view of life, begins. The Bhagavad Gita literally translates as

the 'Song Divine'. It is, however, much more than a
lyric. Its 700 shlokas in eighteen chapters, placed in the
sixth book of the *Mahabharata*, essay a philosophical
outlook of the most profound impact and significance.
The text unfolds in the nature of a dialogue between
Arjuna, caught in the throes of doubt and confusion,
and Krishna, who counsels him in his moment of crisis.
In the end, Arjuna, his mental equilibrium restored and
his sense of futility removed, picks up his bow and arrow
and boldly enters the fight.

The eclectic ideological framework of the Gita
allows for each of its commentators to interpret it from
a subjective perspective, although, inevitably, many such
commentators assert that their interpretation is the only
valid one. The Gita, by its very nature, indulges such
interpretative individualism. Perhaps, therefore, it is
better to comment on the Krishna–Arjuna discourse
from a *personal* frame of reference, from a viewpoint
that derives authenticity because it stems from an
intimacy of experience. To do so does not require one
to have a specialized knowledge of all the philosophical
intricacies that have been tagged on to the Gita. An
amalgamation of all the interpretations of the Gita
would be an exercise in prolix meaninglessness. This is
not to suggest that there is nothing to be learnt from
some of these interpretations. But, ultimately, in the
arena of the human predicament, there has to be

contemplative solitude. And it is how the Gita impacts on the silences that constitute the discrete experience of each person's existential dilemma that gives it enduring meaning and value.

On the battlefield, Arjuna, representing 'generic man', suffered a motivational void. In a flash, all the carefully imbibed 'oughts' of his life crumbled. He was gripped by the sudden realization of the futility of effort, in a world bereft of any ontological meaning. Endeavour and strife have intrinsic value if they are earthed in an explicable context. But to a man who does not know why he is born, and why he will die, the din and fury of the intervening period becomes, at the first moment of corrosive questioning, a pointless pantomime. There is no collective panacea for a man who, in one valid but unguarded instance, comes face to face with his own irrelevance. In a universe, benumbingly vast, with galaxy upon galaxy existing in causeless, mechanical monotony, the individual is dwarfed by his own meaningless finitude. In one blindingly perceptive realization, the conditioned moorings of his life are swept away by the sheer barrenness of the cosmic drift, informing him and everything else in his life. One is born, one lives and one dies. There is no enlightening redemption from the starkness of this sterile charade. And all of a sudden the purport of ambition and achievement, of causes and goals, becomes opaque. And a weariness ensues.

The greatness of the Gita was that it began by portraying this alienation. It recognized the thinking individual's rebellion against the unquestioning acceptance of the validity of effort. Arjuna was not Bheema, whose actions were characterized by temperamental fluctuations; he was also unlike Yudhishthira, whose choice of volition had congenitally subordinated itself to the call of conventional duty. Arjuna's despair had authenticity because it afflicted *him*. The entire burden of his conditioning was to accept battle as his very raison d' être. And yet, being Arjuna, at a crucial moment of his life, he was consumed by doubt about the *value,* in any ultimate sense, of his assumed role.

The aim of Krishna's discourse was to attempt to give purpose and context to the lives of people like Arjuna. The attempt was both adroit and Herculean; adroit because an armada of approaches were employed without scattering the focus of the exercise; and Herculean because the task was nothing less than to salvage for the individual a framework for existence, which would perhaps render palatable—or even help transcend—the essential meaninglessness of his life.

Krishna's first task was to devalue the human condition in its empirical attributes by postulating the infinitude of its essential and non-empirical attribute. It was an efficacious methodology, not because it was

startlingly original, but because the basic Vedantic logic
was put forward with refreshing clarity and as a
pragmatic response to a specific existential situation.
Arjuna could not comprehend an imperative for action
in a phenomenal world that was stubbornly inexplicable.
The Gita partially conceded his point. The world as
perceived prima facie was indeed finite, transient and
bereft of ultimate value. The body would wither away;
friends and relatives were equally perishable; material
wealth was ephemeral; the whole network of mortal
life, unanchored to any larger, enduring reality was a
fleeting ripple in an endless sea of subsistence, and hence
meaningless. But, said Krishna, there is, behind the
bewildering futility of manifest phenomenon, something
else which transcends empirical limitations. This is the
self, the soul, the essential being, Atman, the Supreme
Spirit, the Brahman—call it what you will. The body
may suffer birth and death, but this Self is never born
and does not die. It is indestructible, eternal, unchanging,
immovable, indefinable, unseen and omnipresent.
Arjuna's despondence at the pointlessness of endeavour
in the human realm had validity but only in a constricted
frame of reference. By these terms of reference, he, as a
mere individual, was an infinitesimal irrelevance in an
existence galactic in its aimlessness. But if he could be
persuaded that, unknown to himself, his *essential* self,
was inherently transcendent over the incomprehensible

dross of his perceived existence, then a first step towards the reclamation of purpose in life could be made.

A second step directly related to the first was the assertion that this essential self was, even at the individual level, beyond the clutches of mortality. It is mentioned in the Gita:

> Thy tears are for those beyond tears; and are thy words words of wisdom? The wise grieve not for those who live; and they grieve not for those who die—for life and death shall pass away.
> Because we all have been for all time: I, and thou, and those kings of men. And we all shall be for all time, we all for ever and ever.
> As the Spirit of our mortal body wanders on in childhood, and old age, the Spirit wanders on to a new body: of this the sage has no doubts.
> He is never born, and he never dies. He is in Eternity: he is for evermore. Never-born and eternal, beyond times gone or to come, he does not die when the body dies.

The finality of death renders redundant mortal activity. The thread of life hangs in perpetual dread of the severance of death. Why? What for? To what purpose?—these are the questions which chip away the individual's sense of belief in his own being, when confronted by his irrevocable vulnerability in the face of death. The assertion, therefore, that mortal death is not the final chapter and that each *particular* soul on its way to salvation will reincarnate itself in another body, provides a continuum of perspective that at once imbues with value and meaning the scope of endeavour in this life. It gives to our otherwise puny and insignificant lives a larger canvas. The stage of our human here-and-now endeavours acquires a wider perspective. Our actions acquire intrinsic value for their *quality* will determine the journey that our soul will take in more lives to come. Our karmas in this life will be responsible for the fruits we get in the next. Our actions are thus not forlornly adrift in isolation. At once, we become part of a greater destiny, and the inert vacuum of purpose afflicting our lives is set aside by the breadth of this new vision. Life then becomes not a one-act, vaudeville show abruptly terminated by death, but a more serious business, with questions of purpose and meaning linked to a continuum governed by its own mortality—defying the dynamics of cause and effect.

Within this larger metaphysical framework, the question of how best to interface with the mundane world, with its daily tedium of action and choice, volition and consequence, remains. The Atman or Brahman may be eternally fulfilled, but the individual, even

incorporating in himself an ansh of that transcendent
reality, has to strive to retain equilibrium and balance
reflective of that reality, in the midst of the business of
living. The bulk of the Gita is devoted to essaying a
modus vivendi to answer this seminal existential poser.
The first premise is that in the human realm, involvement
with action in some way or the other is unavoidable.
There cannot be renunciation of action. The Gita is
crystal clear on this.

If action cannot be avoided, then the next question
is how to 'cohabit' with it while retaining one's serenity
and peace of mind. The 'action' in question here is not
that which falls within the purview of mechanical
stimulus and response. It is not an involuntary sequence
of locomotion. The eye blinks, the tympanum vibrates,
the nose twitches. This involuntary action of the motor
nerves is not at the core of the action-in-life which is the
focus of the Gita. The Gita is concerned with action
which is the result of *conscious choice*. It is this locus of
movement which internalizes in itself the potential for
turbulence. This was the source of trauma for Arjuna
on that day of battle. In his own case the canvas was
spectacular: shining banners, the battlefield and
resplendent chariots. But the virus could as easily affect
an ordinary clerk, one ordinary day, as he gets ready to
go to the office: Is the effort justified? Is it required?
What will be its reward? Can it be substituted by another

course of action?

The clamour in action arises when the mental processes interface with the daily vicissitudes of living. This interface is unavoidable, but its consequences are not unalterable. An object, a person, a relationship, a situation, a place becomes important because we give it a certain *value*. The point to consider is to what extent the giving of this value is a necessary and inherent aspect of the human situation.

It would appear that in the praxis of human situations, there is no fixed law of universal cause and effect. For instance, situation A influences person B, but leaves person C unmoved. Now, if there was something inherently value-invoking in situation A in a universally applicable way, then person C would have been influenced with the same intensity as person B. Obviously, if the giving of this value is not an inherent attribute of the situation itself, then its origins must be *in the person himself*. From here arises the next and fundamental question: To what extent can this giving of value be controlled?

The Gita firmly believes that the *value imbuing* process is controllable. Going further, it strongly advocates that in order to overarch the tension and agitation of daily life, the individual should *seek* to control it. The Gita's prescription, in this regard, breathtaking in its simplicity, but undoubtedly based on profound empirical observation, is that action-in-life should be performed free of attachment, sans desire, and, most importantly, *without tainting it with the value of expectation.*

A mindset, acquired through conscious effort and discipline, which delinks the performance of action with a contemplation of its reward is, according to the Gita, an invincible panacea to the strife of daily living. Like much else in the Gita, it is an exhortation based on sound common sense. In the mortal world, involvement in action is unavoidable but it hardly needs reiteration that there is no guaranteed nexus of efficacy between effort and achievement. There are in life too many imponderables and variables that can make the most well planned actions go awry, and the most unintended effort achieve success. Even from the point of pragmatic expediency, an obsession with consequence even as the effort is unfolding, is an inefficient utilization of available energy. Action, which one considers right, should be performed, as an *end in itself*, severing it from the debilitating and ineffectual preoccupation with reward. Then, action, which in the absence of such an approach could agitate, becomes a means to constructively overcome such agitation, an act of consecration, enabling the retention of peace of mind.

But is the ideal of nishkama karma—*desireless* action—really feasible? After all, it appears but natural for an individual to work towards a result, to be conscious of the desired consequence of his efforts, to be seized, in short, of the likely rewards of his endeavours. Does the Gita, therefore, espouse an impracticable behavioural pattern? We are all conscious of our individual identities. Each of us has an ego that strives for recognition and achievement. Can this sense of 'I-ness' this ahankar, this consciousness of 'self' constantly striving for projection in competition with other individual egos, be nullified? The Gita's answer, drawing heavily from the mainstream concepts of Hindu philosophy, is twofold. At one level, it *devalues* the scope of such an ego. 'These warriors,' Krishna tells Arjuna, 'will one day cease to exist *even without you.*' A man who, therefore, thinks that without him, the world around him will collapse, is deluded. In a transient and ephemeral world, there is a finiteness to our preoccupations, and an even greater finiteness to our abilities in configuring them. As Krishna reiterates: 'When a man sees himself as the only agent, he cannot be said to see.' More importantly, our actions, are, in the normal course, far less autonomous than we would like to believe. 'There is no being on earth, or among the Gods in heaven free from the triad of qualities that are born of nature,' Krishna says to Arjuna. Our actions are affected by these inherent qualities of nature, 'but deluded by individuality, the self thinks, "I am the actor."'

At another level, the Gita, as already stated earlier, *exalts* the ego, by claiming that it too is a part of the infinite Atman, the supreme spirit. Once our individual self is assimilated in such an all pervasive entity and elevated to such a transcendent pedestal, then the preoccupation with projecting our own little selves, is logically diminished. The Upanishadic saying, *Tat Twam Asi*—That Thou Art—becomes a three word demolition squad against the normal expectation-ridden, ego-infested way of thinking.

On the methodology of achieving the desired mutation in our attitude towards action, the Gita is, significantly enough, one of the least dogmatic texts in Hindu philosophy. Its overriding purpose is the conquest of mental strife and agitation. It is unambivalently clear on the principle cause of this strife and agitation; but, beyond this, it does not limit its effectiveness by espousing only one path to redemption. For some, jnanamarg, the path of knowledge, in which the real nature of things is understood through the acquisition of knowledge, could be the most efficacious; for others, the path of bhakti or devotion, in which all the fatiguing retention of our misguided individuality is surrendered cataclysmically to the will of the Almighty, could be better; and for others still, the path of karma or action, in which all activity, free from the taint of 'I-ness' or thought of reward, is performed as a daily consecration,

could be the best of all. This exhilarating lack of dogma
in the Gita comes through transparently in the following
stanzas:

> Set thy heart on me alone, and give to me thy
> understanding: thou shalt in truth live in me
> hereafter.
> But if thou art unable to rest thy mind on me,
> then seem to reach me by the practice of Yoga
> concentration.
> If thou art not able to practise concentration,
> consecrate all thy work to me. By doing mere
> action in my service thou shalt attain perfection.
> And if even this thou art not able to do, then
> take refuge in devotion to me and surrender to
> me the fruit of all thy work—with the selfless
> devotion of a humble heart.
> For concentration is better than mere practice,
> and meditation is better than concentration; but
> higher than meditation is surrender in love of
> the fruit of one's actions, for a surrender follows
> peace.

If there is one dominant attribute of the Gita, it is
its advocacy of the harmonious life, as an overriding
goal, valid in itself. Here its analysis is both ruthless
and precise. The onslaught of the senses is forever at

war with a person in pursuit of wisdom and serenity. If the onslaught is not checked, attachment arises, and from attachment, desire; desire leads to anger, and anger to confusion; confusion causes distortions in memory, and such distortion in turn leads to loss of understanding. Once understanding is lost, all is lost. Attraction and repulsion, attachment and hatred, are inherent in any interaction with the phenomenal world, if the senses are not kept in control. To the Gita, desire is the root cause of the loss of serenity. The power of desire is not underestimated; at more than one place the Gita equates it with a voracious fire, capable of devouring the resolve of even the wisest of men. The renunciation of desire is, however, not stated as a religious dictum; its harmful impact is psychologically analysed and its consequences spelt out with clinical elaboration. The man in the grip of desire is bound by a hundred shackles of hope, forever confused by fanciful thoughts, and consumed by pride, anger and greed. In short, desire while initially seductive, is in the long run enslaving, and non-conducive to the peaceful life. It must therefore be vanquished, through a control of the senses. 'Great Warrior,' Krishna exhorts Arjuna, 'kill the enemy menacing you in the form of desire.'

In stark contrast to the discordance and inadequacy of the man without harmony, is the serenity and composure of the sthita prajana, the man who has seen the reality of the world around him and his own role within it, and has his faculties and senses firmly in control. The Gita is most persuasively evocative in portraying the qualities of such a person. He is impartial to joy and sorrow, gain or loss, victory or defeat, failure or success. He neither exults nor hates. He is unmoved in fortune or misfortune, honour or disgrace. He is calm, controlled and poised and possessed of a quietness of mind. Forever content, he is autonomous in his source of delight which is his inner self. He is beyond fear and anger and envy and greed. He has conquered cravings and passion and is free of desires, expectations and vain hopes. At peace with himself, his detachment is imbued with a transparent tranquillity. Imperturbable, unwavering and still, his composure is not shaken by others, while others find peace in his presence. His contemplative calm is suffused by good will for all. His entire demeanour and personality is like a lamp 'whose light is steady for it burns in a shelter where no winds come'. The joy that radiates from his being is effortless, untainted by the strain and tension of denial and discipline.

In its pervasive idealization of the harmonious person, the Gita at one point appears to ride roughshod over issues of social equality and equity. It is of course true that the Gita, while enjoying the reverence due to a religious text, was also a social document, reflecting in

part the prevalent views of thinking of the period when
it was written. The writing of the Gita is generally
ascribed by historians to the period between AD 150 to
AD 350 although there are scholars who have dated it as
far back as 500 BC. It is possible that the text was not
written by one individual but that portions were
additions or accretions by people whose motivation
could very well have also been the preservation and
perpetuation of their class interest. In any case, in Hindu
religious texts, the intrusion by the Brahminical class of
portions which give divine sanction to a social order
congruent with their interests, was not uncommon. It
does seem likely, therefore, that the reference to the four
varnas in the Gita, and its exhortation that the individual
should acquiesce in their inflexible inequity, was included
for such a purpose. Krishna was used as a mouthpiece
for giving divine sanction to entrenched vested interests
representing the Brahmin–Kshatriya coalition. To the
same class would belong the following shloka in section
9: 'For all those who come to me for shelter, however
weak or humble or *sinful* they may be—women or
Vaishyas or Shudras—they all reach the Path supreme.'

The textual chastity of the Gita has been blemished
by such crude attempts to make it a vehicle for social
biases and prejudice. The interpolatory nature of the
attempt is also quite obvious. The shloka cited above
fits in poorly with the general tenor of the section to

which it belongs, and is even more out of place when seen against the totality of the Gita's perspective. More than anything else, to make Sringaramurtimam Krishna pronounce women as 'sinful' is, to say the least, disingenuously laboured, if not patently ludicrous.

This being said, it would be unfair to damn the text as a whole for the unacceptable aberrations of a small segment of it. It is indeed a rare religious text that completely transcends the limitations of the thinking of its time, or is totally oblivious to the social circumstances of the period when it was penned. There is, besides, another aspect to be considered. Perhaps, the Gita was deliberately less than sensitive to notions of social justice and egalitarianism because these concepts, while unquestionably valid in themselves, were not the primary focus of its concern. The Gita was seeking to essay the attributes of a life enduringly free from the viruses of anxiety and tension. Its aim was to give man a panacea for his perpetually destabilizing interaction with the world around him. Given this frame of reference, it is not inconceivable that, for the Gita, *contentment* was a higher goal than the agitation of mind that necessarily accompanies the struggle to change the parameters conditioning our daily existence. Of course, it would be wrong, even for a moment, to postulate that the Gita was consciously articulating a passive acceptance of injustice. Krishna asked Arjuna to pick up his bow and fight because the Kauravas represented injustice. But in motivating him to do so, he appealed to his *duty* as ordained by his vocation in life, namely that of a warrior. He did not tell him to organize a yagna to pray for the defeat of evil, as he would for instance have exhorted a priest to do. Nor did he give him 'revolutionary' advice to give up his status in life to take up the battle through any and whatever means available. To this extent, Krishna was a person of his phenomenal time and place.

But to return to the mainstream context of the Gita. The earth is a minor planet in our solar system. The sun is a minor star amidst the millions of other stars with their own solar systems that form our galaxy. And there are millions of galaxies. The mind-boggling vastness of the universe, the timelessness of time, and the inevitability of creation, still act, for many, as a corrosive to faith. The notion that an individual life has an anchorage of purpose and meaning seems to stray adrift the moment we juxtapose it to the seamless canvas of its background. For those continuing to be assailed by such doubt, Krishna, in the Gita, offered redemption through an assertion of his own all-encompassing divinity. Arjuna, the ever questioning intellect, wanted visible proof of the Absolute to facilitate his quantum leap to faith. Philosophical reasoning and postulations were not sufficient for him. In the tenth and eleventh chapter of the Gita, Krishna fulfilled Arjuna's reverential curiosity. 'I am,' said Krishna, 'not only Vishnu, but also Shiva and all the other Gods; I am the mountain, I am the lake, I am the animal, and I am the bird and the serpent; I am the wind, I am the river, I am the sage, the detached philosopher, as also the God of Love; I am the creator of sound and its articulator, the beginning of time, time itself, and its destroyer. In me are all the human attributes, the rhythm of every melody, the fragrance of every flower, the knowledge of every mystery. In short, I am the beginning, the middle, and the end of all creation, and nothing, animate or inanimate, can exist without me. And, even this elaboration,' he said, 'is not necessary; suffice it to know that the entire universe is pervaded and supported by but a fragment of my Being.'

But Arjuna wanted to *see* to believe. Beyond the theoretical description, he asked Krishna to physically reveal to him his being in all its majestic plenitude. Once again, Krishna complied, giving Arjuna, for that moment, a divine eye to see his glorious form. And Arjuna saw a Being whose radiance was equivalent to that of a thousand suns put together, a form which encapsulated in itself the entire universe, a Body, with innumerable arms and mouths, and eyes which had a glow as powerful as that of the sun and the moon. He saw too all the gods paying obeisance to this magnificent reality, whose beginning or end could not be seen, and in whom burnt the fires of destruction and of the terror of relentless time. In Him, Arjuna saw the past, the present and the future; the Creator, the Preserver and the Destroyer. It was a wondrous experience, exalting as also daunting, and, finally, unable to bear the sheer density and magnitude of the experience, Arjuna implored Krishna to assume again his human form.

God

In Vrindavan, they still believe that every night Krishna and Radha meet to enact their rasa leela. The city is more concrete than jungle, overcrowded and dirty, like so many other cities in India caught in the penumbra of development, neither metropolis nor village. An unexpected expanse of green greets the visitor when he enters Madhuvan, a large walled-in courtyard full of stunted but green amarvraksha trees, remnants, it is said, of the lush grove where Madhu and his beloved met on moonlit nights in sensual dalliance. They say Rang Bhavan—the garden pavilion in the centre of the shrubbery—still has traces every morning of their passionate love play. Betel leaves inexplicably adorn the floor. There is a broken bangle or two. And often also parts of a gajra, the weave of the flower strings undone, but the flowers still in bloom. They say that no man or beast can stray into this garden of love at night. Retribution for encroaching on the privacy of the divine lovers is severe. Those who have tried have been maimed, or robbed of their senses, or rendered deaf and dumb. In nearby Sevakunj, where it is believed Krishna and Radha rest after their rasa, a bed (shayya) decorated with flowers is still prepared every evening. The doors are reverentially locked at night so that none may stray in inadvertently to disturb their rest. And on a sandy stretch along the river Yamuna—the Raman Reti— people still build sand-houses in the hope that the Yugal

Sarkar—Krishna and Radha—strolling hand in hand in the wind-caressed nights, may walk over the edifices, and thus bless them.

Krishna and Radha live on in and around Vrindavan, not as lore or legend but simply as *faith*. Every year, hundreds of devotees happily chant their way on foot on a pilgrims' trail that leads from Mathura to Vrindavan, to Gokul, Nandgaon, Barsana and Goverdhan. Goverdhan, the mountain which Krishna so effortlessly lifted on his little finger, can hardly be seen. It is at best an indifferent hillock, but this hardly tests the faith of the worshippers. They are aware of the belief that the more sin proliferates in the world, the more the mountain is diminished, and they complete the 22 km parikrama of the elevation with gusto. At Goverdhan, there is a water tank. It is said that its waters were brought forth by Krishna by merely scratching the soil with his flute—an art of mental invocation. The Sarovar is thus called Mansi Ganga, and huge crowds gather on its steps during the festival of Diwali.

At Barsana, Radha's village, not far from Vrindavan, the entire area is sprinkled with sites commemorating her love for the blue god. Radha Kund is the pond where she swam with Krishna; Anjanokh is the bower where he lovingly put collyrium in her eyes; Mor Kuti is the spot where he disguised himself as a peacock and danced for her; and Sankhet is the place

where the two met secretly to make love. In the post
monsoonal verdant countryside, people gather also to
celebrate another sport associated with Krishna:
wrestling. The arenas are makeshift, and the audience
is happy to watch from tree perches or tractor tops, but
the enthusiasm is in no way less than what it must have
been when Dau and Mohan took on Kamsa's famed
wrestlers, Chanura and Mustika. In spring, the colourful
if tumultuous festival of Holi is another mass invocation
of the name of Krishna. When Krishna and the gopas
smeared Radha with colour, or when she, with her
sakhis, took Krishna by surprise and drenched him in
coloured water, it was but one aspect of their many-
splendoured love play. The men and women of Braj still
play Holi as though each of them was Krishna or Radha,
a gopa or a sakhi. There is a popular local saying: *Jag
Holi Braj Hola* (The world plays holi; the people of Braj,
hola). A sensuous undercurrent permeates the
celebrations and sometimes, given the social sanction
of this occasion to the public interaction between the
sexes, the latent eroticism is more than overt, a conscious
negation of inhibition in the name of divine precedent.
The animating mythology takes on different forms. At
Barsana, it is *Lathmar* Holi, where the women take sticks
and beat the men who have improvised shields to protect
themselves; at Cirkula, the ladies strip the men of their
clothes, and use the shreds to whip them; in Javgaon,

there is the excitement of the forbidden, as wives play uproarious Holi with their husband's elder brothers. The parallel here is of Radha and Balarama. Masti is a word typical to India and difficult to render in the English language. It is a combination of ecstasy and joy and heedless abandon. They say that during Holi in Braj, masti was at such a peak that Balarama abandoned the restraint normally expected of an elder, and played Holi with Radha, who too jettisoned the customary reserve of the bahu, the daughter-in-law. Balarama has been profiled as the strong, earthy, uncomplicated, gentlemanly hedonist. His Holi was horanga, famed for its vigour and lack of inhibition. Fond of wine, his Bacchanalian exploits included dragging Yamuna, the river, by her hair closer to himself to quench his thirst. The bend in the river, at Ramghat, is attributed to this tantrum. At Baldevgaon, close to Vrindavan, there is a temple where he is worshipped along with his consort Revati. On Holi, devotees gather and offer cannabis to him and there is much rakish revelry in evidence.

Rasa leela, amateur theatre, enacting incidents from the life of Krishna, draws huge crowds in Braj, particularly during the days preceding Janamashtami. The rasacharyas of Vrindavan are respected doyens of this local theatrical tradition. Their repertoire includes over a hundred rasa leela plays, covering mostly Krishna's life from birth to the slaying of Kamsa—

Kamsa vadha. Devotees reach the Ram-Mandap—open air theatrical arenas—in the evening, having spent the day completing the ritual ablutions (snana), prayer (puja) and worship at the temple (murti darshan). The microphones are often faulty, the actors hardly professionally rehearsed, but the mood is devotional, with spontaneous public participation in the singing, dancing and music. And when, in the midst of the play, the actor and actress playing the roles of Krishna and Radha are brought out in tableau (jhanki), the spectators offer monetary offerings to them, seeing in this human portrayal the reflection of the divine.

At the famous temple of Nathdwara, near Udaipur in Rajasthan, Krishna is worshipped as Shrinathji—Lord of Shri. The entire worship in the temple is premised on the assumption that the image of Krishna in the sanctum sanctorum is living. Shrinathji is ceremonially woken up every morning—the mangala darshan—and actually offered a light breakfast, consisting of fruits, and his favourite—butter. A little later in the day, during the sringara darshan, he is, as part of prescribed ritual, shown a mirror to check his appearance and a flute is placed in his hands. The gwala darshan, where he is dressed as a cowherd, coincides with the time when he would have taken the cows out to graze. In the afternoon, the temple is closed for a while, for it is his time of rest. Following the siesta, devotees can see him being offered the afternoon meal. The last darshan is just before he sleeps and some food is left by the side of his bed, in case he feels hungry at night. His clothes change according to the time of the day and season of the year. At the height of summer, he is given a ceremonial bath. The Snana Yatra—bathing festival— is a popular occurrence. Srinathji is lovingly placed in a silver chariot and taken out in procession. This is the time when the mangoes have come to fruit, and an offering of 25,000 of the best of the harvest is offered to the god who makes no secret of his love for the good things of life. In the adjacent states of Gujarat and Maharashtra, the monsoon sees the Jal Jhilani festival, which celebrates the bathing of the cowherds in the rain. When the clouds gather, Krishna is set out in the open and bathed with his young friends in the rain amidst a great deal of fun and revelry.

Across the land from Udaipur, at Puri, on the eastern coast, Krishna is worshipped as Jagannath—Lord of the world. The Jagannath temple at Puri is an extremely important centre of Krishna worship. The image of Krishna here shows definite tribal influence and the iconography is unusual in that he is flanked by his sister, Subhadra, and brother, Balarama. As in Nathdwara, Jagannathji is ceremonially bathed in May or June, but what is interesting is that after the Snana Yatra is over, the deities are kept in a sick chamber for fifteen days out of public view as they are said to have contracted fever from bathing at midday! The most famous festival at Puri is the Rath Yatra—the Car Festival. Every year in June or July, Jagannathji is placed in a wooden chariot and taken to his summer residence—the Gundicha temple some 3 km away. The chariot is pulled by over 4000 special coolies—the kalebetiyas—who enjoy hereditary concessions in neighbouring villages for this service. The distance is short but such are the vast crowds that the journey can take up to three or four days. A sea of humanity greets the eye and there is much vociferous if benevolent confusion, and even greater devotional fervour, as each devotee seeks to contribute to the pulling of the chariot.

The Jhoolan Yatra, the festival of swings, is another popular celebration in Puri. In the month of July or August, an icon of Krishna, along with Radha, is placed on a swing gaily decorated with images of dancing girls and musicians made of paper or metal foil. The swing is gently swayed by a relay of priests while goti puas, young boys dressed as girls trained to dance professionally, dance to the lyrics of Jayadeva's *Gitagovinda*. In Nathdwara, a similar swinging ceremony—the Phul Dol—takes place in February or March. The image of Krishna as Navanitapriyaji—the child on all fours crawling with a ball of butter in his hand—is placed on a flower-bedecked swing and rocked reverentially.

Each ritual is wrapped in its own myth, its own 'mythologized' kernel of history encased in its own specificities of devotion. An interesting legend relates to the establishment of the Guruvayoor temple, deep in the south of the subcontinent, in the lush green state of Kerala. On the eve of his death, Krishna entrusted an image of Narayana, which he used to worship himself, to his friend Uddhava, who in turn gave it, in safekeeping, to the Guru of the Gods—Brihaspati, who, assisted by his disciple Vayu, brought it to its present location, where Shiva himself consecrated the installation. Hence the name: Guruvayoor.

The murti at Guruvayoor is considered by many to be the most resplendent. Krishna is dressed in a robe of yellow silk, with a shining crown on his head. The disc, the conch, the mace and the lotus can be seen in his four hands. Ornamental drops glisten in his ears, the vanamala garland adorns his neck and the lustrous kausthubha jewel rests on his chest. Shri, the Goddess of Prosperity, and Dhara, the Goddess of Earthly Wealth, hold him on either side in loving embrace. His face is in smiling repose. An unending stream of devotees throng the temple. Hundreds of children are brought every day for their first feed of cereal—annaprasam. Dozens of couples are married in its precincts daily, for it is believed that this ensures a happy marital life. The Guruvayoor Utsava (festival) takes place in February or March and lasts for ten days. The entire township appears spruced up for the event—houses are white-washed, fencing and tiles repaired, and the streets along which the procession will pass festooned with arches and ornamentation. A distinctive feature of the festival is the avoidance of loud fire-crackers, for these are likely to frighten Unnikrishna—the boy Krishna. The celebrations are a visible community event, with the multitudes thoroughly enjoying the daily engagements, culminating in a mass dip in the temple-tank, and an elephant chase, whose din and furore and devotional ecstasy is said to have a miraculous curative impact on patients suffering from rheumatism and paralysis. Within the temple structure there hangs today the photograph of the great vocalist Chembai Vaidhyanatha Bhagavatha. It is said that in 1938 he was to give a performance at the Zamorin's palace at Calicut but people were amazed to see that not a sound came from his silently moving lips. Chembai rushed to Guruvayoor and craved the mercy of the Lord. Miraculously, his voice was restored.

But who could confine Braj Bihari within the confines of a temple? As he had danced with Radha in the groves of Vrindavan and, as the notes of his flute had wafted beyond the groves to be carried along the ripples of the Yamuna, so did he dance and sing and paint his way into the lives of the common folk in a hundred enticing ways. He was Akhila Kaladi Guru—

the apostle of all arts and the embodiment of all that
was beautiful. It is believed that all the arts emanated
from his dance on the hood of the serpent Kaliya. In
that moment of creative rhythm, beautiful in its frenzied
control, subtle in its balance, and unparalleled in the
vigour of its impact, poetry was born, and taala, and
poetry in movement. If Shiva, in the awesome grandeur
of his tandava was Nataraja, Krishna, in the delicate
seduction of his movements, was Natwara. He is the
main theme of the Manipuri dance of the north-east, of
Kathak in the north, and of Odissi in Orissa. In
Karnataka, the Yakshagana dance form celebrates his
aishvarya bhava, the heroic exploits of the Chakravartin
Krishna; in Andhra, the Kuchipudi dance style relives
his daring theft of the Parijata tree for Satyabhama; and
in Tamil Nadu, he is one of the main subjects of the
classical Bharatnatyam dance. In Kerala, Prince
Manavendra wrote eight dramas on Krishna, drawing
from the *Gitagovinda* and the Bhagavata Purana. From
the plays was born the dance form of Krishnaattam—
the dance of Krishna, a forerunner of the more popular
Kathakali. In Gujarat, the more folksy Lakuta and
Dandiya rasa are inspired by him; and, in Maharashtra,
the vibrant Tamasha folk theatre depicts with abandon
his audacious dan leela. In Assam, we have the local
dramatic tradition of the Ankia nat and the immensely
popular plays of Srimanta Sankaradeva, the great saint-

reformer of the fifteenth century. Sankaradeva was a great devotee of Krishna. His collection of poems—*Kirtana Ghosh*—is regarded as the most sacred religious book by the Hindus in Assam. He wrote six dramas of which five were on Krishna. In Bengal, the Chaitanya-inspired yatra dramas are extremely popular, and in the tribal belt of Chattisgarh, the Jhumar songs and Rahas dance, celebrating the love of Krishna and Radha, keep improvised gatherings enthralled the entire night, night after night.

Krishna's presence in music is equally ubiquitous. In Bengal, they have a saying: *Kanu bina gita nahin* (without Krishna there is no song). He is the focus of the largest numbers of compositions in Indian classical music and his presence is even more pervasive in the light classical music genre of the thumri, raas, hori, dadra and charchari songs. Indeed, most thumris are written in Braj bhasha, the language of the Krishna bhakti cult. In a way, the thumri, akin to the khayal ang of Hindustani music, but much more relaxed and without the self-consciousness of its more stringent classical elder, was a particularly apt medium to relate to Krishna. Its bol was not in rhetorical Sanskrit or stylized Urdu; its compositions reflected the simplified language of the heart, the outpourings of musicians rather than grammarians. Thumri after thumri deals evocatively with the pangs of separation from Krishna. Radha asks:

Bata de Sakhi, Kiun gali gayo Shyam? (Tell me friend, through which alleyway did Shyam go?); or vexed by Shyam's *barjori* she says: *Kanha mori gagariya phori re, Dekho, dekho re langarva ne kinhi barjori* (Kanha, broke my earthen pot, see how the mischievous one has behaved with me); or plaintively she implores him: *Chunariya de de mori Shyam, Bar bar kar jorat tum son* (Give me my scarf Shyam, again and again I plead with folded hands); or sometimes, in an ecstasy of longing, she bursts out:

> *Tum Radha bano Shyam*
> *Sab dekhenge brij bama*
> *Sab Sakhiyan mili natch nachave*
> *Yeh hai brij ghan Shyam.*

> You come dressed as Radha, Shyam,
> All the women will watch,
> And sing and dance
> This is the dark as clouds Shyam.

In the hands of musical wizards like Faiyaz Khan, Bade Ghulam Ali, Rasoolan Bai, Siddheswari Devi and Begum Akhtar—to name but a few—such simple lines acquired an emotional luminosity that could be profoundly moving, full of sweetness, with a certain sensuous pathos, and yet retaining the robustness and lack of inhibition of their essentially folk origins.

The many forms of Krishna, particularly his roop as a child and a lover, and the many incidents and events related to these two forms, were irresistible material for the visual artist as well. The Bhagavata, the *Harivamsa* and the *Gitagovinda* were illustrated because their written content unleashed a canvas of imagery—part imagination part fantasy—that cried out to be given visual form. The tidal wave of output came in the sixteenth century when poets like Surdas, Keshav Das and Bihari took the Krishna theme by storm. Although the poems of Surdas and Bihari were favourite material for the painters, it is not surprising that Keshav Das's sensual eroticism was responsible for the greatest number of illustrations. The princely states in Rajasthan and Himachal Pradesh were the centres of this Krishna related renaissance in Indian painting. Krishna's sringara roop was the dominant theme but popular incidents of his childhood—the lifting of Goverdhan, Kaliyadehan, the killing of Putana, and the stealing of butter—were also portrayed. Krishna became a living icon in the hands of these craftsmen, who embellished his image according to local need and context, for as a personal god his profile could change almost from district to district. In Udaipur, Shrinathji; in Kota, Shri Brajnathji; and in Kishangarh, Kalyan Rai. But beyond his formal form as deity, he was an *ideal,* an *image,* a *concept,* that could be moulded to suit the personal needs of a patron and his sensitive master-artist. For instance, in the paintings made by Nihalchand, the famous chef de atelier of Savant Singh, the Raja of Kishangarh, Krishna looks uncannily like the latter, and Radha like Bani Thani, Savant Singh's widely renowned mistress. A similar process, with a few variations in nuance was under way in the Rajput states of Mewar, Malwa and Bundelkhand. In Himachal Pradesh, a virtual efflorescence in Krishna-inspired paintings took place in Basohli under Raja Kripal (1678–95) and his talented son Dhiraj Pal (1695–1725); in Guler under Goverdhan Chand (1744–73); and in Kangra under Raja Sansar Chand (1775–1809). Significant work was also done in Chamba, Kulu, Mandi and Garhwal. In both the hills and in Rajasthan, this school of painting, which gave new vitality to the Moghul miniaturist tradition, unfortunately declined in the nineteenth century with the coming of the British and the advent of the Company School of painting.

In other parts of India, beyond the confines of formal or stylized art, Krishna continued to be an inspiring motif for both devotee and artist alike. In Bengal and Orissa, he was depicted on palm leaves, and in Calcutta, the so-called Kalighat school of paintings catered in particular to pilgrims. In Rajasthan, he was painted on cloth in colours derived from vegetable dyes—the Pichhavai paintings—which have acquired new found popularity in recent times. In Bihar, he was the focus of the vibrant Madhubani folk art, and in Maharashtra and Karnataka, the Paithen paintings specialized in projecting him in his roop as Chakravartin. The now much in vogue Thanjavur paintings (paintings of Tanjore in Tamil Nadu), were first commissioned by rich patrons in the seventeenth century. Traditionally, the artists were the Kshamyas of the Raji community. The medium was wood or glass inscribed over with gold and silver leaf and semi-precious gems. Krishna, particularly Navanita Krishna, was the most pervasive preoccupation of the artists. It is a matter of some interest that Krishna was not the most popular subject in Indian sculpture. Perhaps the less pliable mediums of stone, copper or bronze lent themselves less to the kaleidoscopic variations of the Krishna theme. There are, of course, a few extant pieces of the most exquisite beauty, in both copper and bronze, of the crawling Krishna with a ball of butter in his hand, or of the dancing Krishna—and a few surviving stone panels depicting well-known incidents of Krishna's life; but on the whole it is the more pliable aspects of the Krishna myth which seem to have thrived. Stone and metal create icons of worship for placing on a pedestal. Krishna was ready to be appropriated, to mould himself to the flights of imagination of his followers. He pirouetted effortlessly on an upheld musical note, leapt gracefully out of a painting, and danced in unison to our internal mental rhythms. Peasant or prince, lover or warrior, child or sage, his was à la carte devotional menu. Above all, he was both the embodiment and the sanction of joy. In portraying him, artists revelled in the sheer joyous flexibility of expression he made possible. Hence we notice that even in secular themes, such as that of the Baramaasa series, or the Ragamala paintings, the male figure is that of Krishna.

Indeed, in many respects, Krishna was not just a Hindu deity. His appeal transcended religious boundaries or regional affiliations. Guru Nanak, the founder of the Sikh faith, sang evocatively: 'He Govinda He Gopal,' and the Sikh Shabad kirtans are replete with references to Madho and Shyam. Mian Tansen, the celebrated Muslim court musician of Akbar, could sing with fervour: *Shyam Ghanshyam umad ghumad ayo hai* (Shyam, the dark one, comes circling like the monsoon clouds); and a panoply of renowned Muslim vocalists have continued to sing with joy and familiarity of the dark one. Nawab Wajid Ali Shah, the talented last king of Oudh, wrote two plays titled *Kissa Radhe Kanhaiya Ka* (The story of Radhe and Kanhaiya); when staged, he used to play the part of Krishna himself. The number of Muslims who painted on Krishna themes was significant. In the court of the seventeenth century princely states of Mewar, the master painter who illustrated the Bhagavata Purana was a Muslim,

Sahibdin. At about the same time, Syed Ibrahim Ras
Khan, wrote his *Rachnavali* in praise of Krishna. Its
opening lines were:

> Worthy to be human, are only those Ras Khan,
> Who dwell among the cowherders of Gokul Gaon,
> And blessed alone are those animals,
> Taken to graze with the cows of Nanda's barn.

In Orissa, to this day, devotees sing the Muslim poet
Salbeg's lyrics to welcome Lord Jagannath. And the
image of Krishna is a recurring theme in the outpourings
of Malik Mohammad Jaise, the author of the first great
epic in Avadhi.

A certain eclecticism, a revolt against stifling
narrowness, has been an important element of the
Krishna cult. The very exuberance of Krishna's
personality militated against a very formalized, rigid,
exclusive or hierarchical structure of worship. Ecstasy
rather than dogma, fervour rather than bigotry, and
bhakti rather than shuddhi, have been the dominant
traits of Krishna worship, in accordance with the
defining parameters of the Bhakti and Sufi movements
as a whole. The Bhagavata Purana had laid the basis
for such an approach when it stated categorically: 'I
believe that even a Brahmin equipped with twelve
qualities (wealth, family status, knowledge, yoga,

intellect, etc.) who has turned his face away from the lotus feet of god (Krishna) is inferior to the chandala (outcaste) who has laid his mind, speech, work, wealth and life at god's feet; that chandala saves his whole family, while the Brahmin, arrogant of his station, cannot even save himself.' Not surprisingly, there is very little reference throughout Krishna's sojourn in Vrindavan to traditional Hindu society. In Vrindavan, Braj happily coexists with Bengali as the second most important language of the area. Mathura, where Krishna was born, was, and to some extent still is, an important area for the Jain and Buddhist faiths. The Govindji Temple in Vrindavan, built in AD 1590, has a Hindu elevation, a Christian ground plan and a roof of modified Saracenic character. The musical entourage of one of the most well-known Kathak exponents of the rasa has a Muslim vocalist, a Muslim percussionist and a Muslim sarodist. These are random examples but they are definitive pointers to the basic catholicity of the Krishna faith.

In India, Krishna lives on not only as a symbol of faith, but as a reflex and unquestioned presence in the daily lives of millions of people, a participant in their hopes and joys, sorrows and grief, in their song and dance and music and creative pursuits, in festivals and ceremonials, in laughter and gaiety. In a sense his multilayered personality mirrors the harmonious

schizophrenia of the Hindu mind, which effortlessly
operates at two apparently dichotomous levels—one of
make-believe, ritual, rampant mythology and love, and
the other transcendent, beyond categories, serene in the
realization of the metaphysical unity of divinity. It is
not uncommon to see in a representative Hindu home a
picture of Krishna surrounded by nude women gazing
passionately at him, and another picture of him giving
upadesha to Arjuna on the imperatives of quenching
desire and understanding the self within. To a foreigner,
the diversity of godly attributes in *one* divine persona
could well appear bizarre, but not so to the Hindu, who,
forever conscious at one level of Krishna's celestial status,
has nevertheless joyously—even extravagantly—
humanized him within the framework of his mortal
world. It is only when conscious of such a perspective
that one can understand why in the temple of Jagannath
at Puri, devotees are free to loudly *abuse* Krishna. It is
an aggressive yet overt gesture of proprietary familiarity.
There is a personal bond of intimacy between worshipper
and deity that defies conventional logic. I have been told
that until recently, and perhaps even today in many parts
of India, particularly northern India, young widows
would be given a laddoo Gopal—an image of the child
Krishna—to adopt. The image, of metal or clay, would
then become a living child and the lady would be
absorbed in the daily routine of bringing up *her* Gopal.

It was an activity not very different from playing with a doll. However, significantly enough, other members of the household would view this preoccupation as quite normal. If the lady was busy, a visitor would be told without hesitation: she is busy bathing Gopalji, or she is busy feeding Thakurji! Krishna seemed to enjoy this appropriation. There is a popular story of a devotee who looked upon Krishna as his own child, but was one day overcome by the divine status of his ward; at that moment his feelings changed from filial love to overawed servitude; when this happened, Krishna disappeared, reprimanding his devotee about his flawed perspective: Krishna would be his only so long as he considered him his own.

Much in India has changed today, and the process of transition is still ongoing. Mobility, economic opportunity, industrialization, the widening of the political base and the impact of the mass media, have set adrift old traditions, customs and habits, without as yet another set of enduring beliefs to replace them. The metamorphosis is most clearly in evidence in the bigger cities, where the 'new' culture is described best by the absence of cultural content, a nondescript if more egalitarian drift whose most recognizable element is a gross and increasingly aggressive materialism. The manner in which Krishna survives in this new milieu is yet to be seen. A generation earlier, Janamashtami was celebrated with commitment by the entire extended family, with the children in particular spending days absorbed in building a tableau to recreate the ambience of the place of his birth; today Janamashtami often comes and goes without the younger generation being aware of its advent, and certainly quite ignorant about the manner of its celebration. The cause for this is almost certainly because of new challenges, new goals, and the greater burden of survival in a vastly more competitive environment.

But, it would appear, for all of this, Krishna will survive. Perhaps it is the neurosis of these uncertain times that the numbers of those flocking to his temples show no signs of decrease. Or perhaps his legacy, through a process of osmosis thousands of years old, has been assimilated so imperceptibly by a people that it cannot be mutated without the Hindu psyche itself undergoing a major cataclysmic change. Perhaps, with a twinkle in his eye, he has himself shown a divine agility to change according to the times. For, are there not devotees today in distant and strange lands—the USA, Australia, Russia, Europe and elsewhere—who have given up their own faiths to chant reverentially, 'Hare Rama Hare Krishna' and build temples in his honour and ashrams in his name that seek to recreate Gokula and Vrindavan? And so the saga of his rasa goes on every day (nitya rasa), through all the seasons, in spring (basanta rasa), and in autumn (kunj rasa), and then in that full moon night in early winter, the night of the maharasa, when, in spite of ourselves, everything in the cosmos halts, to dance once again to the magic of his eternal leela.

Bibliography

Bahadur, K.P. (trans) *Bihari, The Satasai* (New Delhi, 1990)

Basham, A.L. *The Wonder that was India* (Delhi, 1971)

Bhattacharya, D. *Love Songs of Chandidasa* (London, 1967)

Bhattacharya, D. (trans) *Love Songs of Vidyapati*, W.G. Archer (ed) (Delhi, 1987)

Byrant, Kenneth E. *Poems to the Child God* (Berkeley, 1978)

De, S.K. *Krishnakarnamrita* (Dacca, 1983)

Dimock, Jr., E. and D. Levertov (eds) *In Praise of Krishna, Songs from the Bengali* (New York, 1967)

Gupta, T.R.C. *Sri Krishna, A Socio-Political and Philosophical Study* (Delhi, 1987)

Hardy, Friedhelm *Viraha-Bhakti: The Early History of Krishna Devotion in South India* (New Delhi, 1983)

Hawley, J.S. *Surdas, Poet, Singer, Saint* (Delhi, 1982)

Hawley, J.S. *Krishna, The Butter Thief* (Princeton, 1983)

Hiltebeitel, Alf 'Krishna at Mathura' in *Mathura: the Cultural Heritage*, Doris Meth Srinivasan (ed) (New Delhi, 1989)

Hutchinson, Francis G. *Young Krishna* (New

Hampshire, 1980)

Mascaro, Juan *The Bhagavad Gita* (UK, 1962)

Mascaro, Juan (trans) *The Upanishads* (London, 1965)

Mukhopadhyay, Durgadas *In Praise of Krishna* (Delhi, 1990)

Munshi, K.M. *Krishnavtara, Volume I* (London, 1951; Reprint Delhi, 1988)

Munshi, K.M. *Krishnavatara, Volume II: The Wrath of an Emperor* (Bombay, 1988)

Narayan, R.K. *The Mahabharata* (Delhi, 1978)

Randhawa, M.S. *Kangra Paintings on Love* (New Delhi, 1962)

Redington, James D. *Vallabhacharya on the Love Games of Krishna* (Delhi, 1983)

Seigel, Lee *Sacred and Profane Dimensions of Love in the Indian Tradition as Exemplified in the 'Gitagovinda of Jayadeva'* (Delhi, 1978)

Subramanian, Kamala *Srimad Bhagavatam* (Bombay, 1979)

Subramanian, Kamala *The Mahabharata* (Bombay, 1982)

Wilkings, W.J. *Hindu Mythology* (London, 1882; Reprint Delhi, 1983)

Wilson, H.H. (trans) *Vishnu Purana* (London, 1840; Reprint Calcutta, 1972)